HUNTER'S TRACKS

HUNTER'S TRACKS

J. A. HUNTER

ASSISTED BY

ALAN WYKES

Safari Press Inc.
P. O. Box 3095, Long Beach, CA 90803

Hunter, J. A.

Safari Press, Inc.

1999, Long Beach, California

ISBN 1-57157-121-3

Library of Congress Catalog Card Number: 58-6205

10 9 8 7 6 5 4 3 2 1

Readers wishing to receive the Safari Press catalog, featuring many fine books on big-game hunting, wingshooting, and sporting firearms, should write to Safari Press Inc., P.O. Box 3095, Long Beach, CA 90803, USA. Tel: (714) 894-9080 or visit our Web site at www.safaripress.com.

DEDICATION

To Hilda, my wife,
whose steadfast loyalty and devoted love have been with me
through all the hunting years.

CONTENTS

MANHUNT I

THE CLUE

THIS time it was a manhunt.

Hardy and I stood on a rise of sand looking across the plateau. From this point a world of desolation stretched before us. Strangely, for the plateau was irrigated by countless streams and watercourses, nothing grew but a few stunted thorn bushes, and even these were grey and brittle from lack of nourishment. The wood snapped dryly as you broke it off, and as you scuffed the pale sandy soil with your feet it rose lightly like a vapour and settled on the sapless bushes—the slow thin powdering of ultimate obliteration. Nothing had time to root properly here. The soil shifted constantly, as if the whole plateau was being tilted sideways, crumbled away from roots that had seized no proper hold, leaving them naked under the shrivelling sun. Sometimes as you watched an immense shifting of soil would begin. No sound; but there would be a sudden hollowing of the ground before you, as if you were watching the level of salt in an inverted salt cellar, and a crater would appear, measuring perhaps a hundred yards across and with the skeleton form of a dead thorn at the bottom of the hole to mark what not so long ago had been an eminence with the thorn crowning the summit. Here, between Kitui and the Athi River, there could be no reliance on the landmarks of contour or stream. Even a watercourse was likely to be diverted or dammed before you returned. The sun streamed down on this arid bit of the Yatta Plateau and was absorbed immediately. Nothing was given back by the earth—no shimmer of heat, no silicate flicker of light from the dead sand, nothing. Hardy and I might have come into the plains of Canaan where some mighty battle had gone by. Yet when we shaded our eyes and looked across the plateau we could see trees and the huts of a village no more than a mile away; and behind us the International truck stood comfortingly on the track, its radiator steaming gently.

But behind that again a herd of buffaloes watched us with sinister curiosity. The buffaloes moved no nearer. They weren't wary of the desolation that lay across these few acres, nor of us. It seemed rather that they were in league with some intangible force we hadn't yet identified. Their hump-shouldered ruminations as they watched us expressed a sneering and triumphant evaluation of whatever it was eluded us. They knew; they knew only too well that we felt the secret urgency that borders upon fear. They knew also—or seemed, in the bovine intensity of their watching, to know only too well—the cause of our apprehension. Which was more than we did. And the unreasoning fear is always the worst.

Hardy and I looked at each other. There were rifles and ammunition in the truck; we needed no assurance on that score. But in any case, as I have said, this was a manhunt; we intended no death nor were we the object of any man's desperation—not that we knew of. There were certainly no beasts to attack us; in any case it is rare for beast to attack man unprovoked. The buffaloes would never attack unless themselves maddened by the death of one of their number. But the silent lifelessness of the plateau was uneasily conspiratorial. Surrounded by an empty waste in which no enemy could have hidden we nonetheless glanced warily around while the beasts with their bow-shaped horns continued to watch us with oppressive contempt.

Then, a couple of hundred yards ahead, there was a movement. A buzzard rose slowly into the air, the beat of its wings clearly audible in the stillness.

The flight of the bird, which circled now above us with wings scarcely moving, had broken the tension. We got into the truck and drove on down the track. It was by chance rather than deliberation that Hardy glanced at the spot where the buzzard had risen. We had no reason for inspecting or identifying the bird's meal. Snake, toad, lizard, frog, carrion—it might have been anything. But Hardy looked and saw that the buzzard had in fact been feasting on carrion: a fair-sized carcass.

'Baboon,' Hardy said. 'Pull up a minute; there's something . . .'

We both got down and walked across to the carcass. It was a baboon all right—full-grown, male. The eyes had been gouged and the flesh shredded by buzzards and vultures. Inside the shell a seething movement of termites was going on. From the rotting flesh that still clung to the chest bones an arrow protruded—a native arrow with the barb tipped with poison.

The natives of the village ahead of us evidently killed, illegally, with poisoned arrows.

'That's where we'll trace our man,' I said.

'We'll need a bit more evidence than that.'

We would, of course. The killing of game by poisoned arrows goes on all the time. You catch the natives and fine them a goat or a bushel of wheat and warn them. They accept the sentence impassively and go on hunting elephants. The rewards for poached ivory are by native standards considerable. They have only to find a buyer in one of the small towns. This they do through a chain of contact men, each of whom will demand a commission; even so the profits remain worthwhile. After a time the poaching natives, in common with so many other human beings, become greedy: they draw attention to

themselves by their affluence, become careless and shoot
elephants too near their villages. Too many and too near.
The carcasses, left to the predatory beasts of the forest, are
still marked by the evidence of the bones; and the storage
of the ivory presents an even greater problem, for tusks,
once extracted, quickly soften and decompose if exposed
to heat and air. And it is not always easy for the natives
to make contact with their buyer quickly. So some kind
of hideout, some cache for the burial of the ivory, is
necessary. It was for such evidence as this that Hardy and
I were looking. Then the hunt for the buyer could really
begin. He would doubtless have to be traced through a
long line of bribed informers; and almost certainly he
would turn out to be one of the Indian storekeepers in
some riverside settlement. Poached ivory always begins
its journey to India in a *dhow* hired by the buyer who
conceals his prosperous smuggling activities behind the
façade of a store filled with junk. Half the time I suspect
that they enjoy the Buchanesque adventures they become
involved in with Game Rangers, just as they enjoy
haggling. It is no part of a Game Ranger's job to ad-
minister justice, but I often get called in—as I had been
called in by Hardy the District Officer—to help with the
accumulation of evidence; and rightly, since the sale and
export of ivory is controlled by the government. If it
weren't so controlled elephants would soon become
extinct. Control of the sale of ivory means, *ipso facto*,
control of the killing of elephants; and it is there that the
Game Ranger comes into the picture, for sometimes,
when elephants cause extensive damage, as they often do,
he must kill; and at other times—when, for example,
extensive poaching is going on—he must help to prevent
killing.

Evidently Hardy and I had found the village where the
poachers had their headquarters. The dead baboon was
in itself unimportant; but the evidence of the poisoned

arrow was significant. Some arrow-happy native had given us just the lead we needed.

We needed more than that, though. A simple arrest and subsequent fine for using poisoned arrows would be easy enough: and nothing would please the natives more than to have everything settled so amicably. But from our point of view it wouldn't settle anything. Blandly the natives would watch us depart—the one who had been fined waving and beaming as happily as the rest—and the poaching would go on. This Wakamba tribe would smilingly (and rather charmingly) deny any guilt in the face of incontrovertible evidence; as for truthful answers to questions—whether these were straightforward or subtly posed to gain admission of guilt—you might as well save your breath. The only thing is to produce evidence acceptable to the D.C.'s representative, who applies the usual principle of British justice—that the accused, whether individual or whole tribe, is innocent until proved guilty.

We didn't find the cache for three days. We hung about the village and its silent environs, talking animatedly with the natives, watching, and being watched. I have never been so powerfully aware of being watched. Yet it was always out on the empty plateau that this apprehension was strongest. In the village the natives came and went, eyeing us with smiles that were perhaps a little too wide; but out on the plateau we had the feeling that something even less tangible than a false smile was mocking us.

Establishing camp in the truck, which we parked under the trees that edged on to the village, we observed the comings and goings of the natives. We watched the clock round between us, taking it in turns to sleep. The natives were not likely to continue their poaching while we were hanging about their village; but we were hoping for some sign of betrayal—some messenger departing to warn an intermediary in another village, perhaps an attempt to conceal the cache which might be plainly visible if we should chance to stumble on it.

Watching at night, in the silence.

It was the silence that irked me. Africa is full of sounds. I'd sat all night in many a hideout waiting for this, that or the other creature to disclose its presence and been entertained by a full orchestra of gibberings, paddings to and fro, screams, coughs, distant trumpetings and the like, some far, some near. But here at the edge of the plateau nothing stirred. The dead soil stretched away in the moonlight like a dream of Armageddon. It unnerved me a little, I admit it. Where everything could be seen there was nothing to see: just the bones and seething scraps of flesh of a dead baboon fifty or so yards away in the moonlight, and my own tracks across the plateau— the tracks of a hunter with nothing, at the moment, to hunt.

Well, at times we all live vicariously in other people's adventures or the memories of our own. This was such a time. Just sitting and thinking, or just sitting, as in the old *Punch* joke, is not for me: I like to be pitting my wits, my sight, my hearing against those of animals. I didn't like the quiet solitude, the knowledge that this time it was a manhunt, that the dishonest brains of men were considering Hardy and me and what we should do and what they would do to preserve the secrecy of their machinations. No: I didn't like any part of the job; but it had to be done.

So on this first night in the silent moonlight, lacking immediate adventures I recalled earlier ones. Imagination isn't my strong point, but the little I possess served me well; and my memory of events since 1908—when I first came to Kenya—and all to do with that fatal year may be relied upon. There isn't much I forget, or want to forget, about Africa.

BABOONS

THE pierced and rotting carcass of the baboon, with my own tracks leading up to it, reminded me that my last assignment before this one had been to help dispatch marauding baboons from a sisal estate at Kibwezi, sixty or so miles south of where I now sat smoking my pipe and waiting for some sign that would start our manhunt rolling.

Baboons are among the worst destroyers of sisal and maize crops. They descend in hundreds on the crowns of sisal on which the young leaves thrive, breaking and destroying them and leaving hundreds of square yards of hand-grown crops pillaged and ruined. Their organized thefts on the maize crops have to be seen to be believed. I have many times seen carefully deployed platoons of baboons converge on a maize-field that has been left unguarded by natives for a short time. At some pre-arranged signal from the leader of the tribe they swing in from the surrounding trees or rocky plateau and with a frenzy of gibberings building up to a Babelish crescendo sweep through the field gathering the cobs of maize as they go. In a few minutes one sees the grotesque figures with their long snouts and horridly naked buttocks swing back again to their rocky eminences, each with a bundle of five or six cobs tucked between forearm and body. Their speed and numbers preclude any possibility of dealing with them except by scaring them off before they attack or by wholesale poisoning methods. Poisoning— by baiting the cobs with sugar coating and then sub-stituting some quick lethal poison—has so far been most successful. But occasionally the farmers or administrators have some success with other methods—as you shall see.

When I was asked to lend a hand at Kibwezi I recalled a method of getting rid of baboons used by Cullen, who'd been employed on this very estate some years previously.

Cullen was a man of great good humour and observation who had made—necessarily, since their depredations on his crops threatened his livelihood—a special study of baboons. It was he who claimed that they should be outlawed and that tourists should be given every encouragement to practise shooting them with unlimited supplies of ammunition.

'They've got a wonderful intelligence, cunning—call it what you like; but their nuisance value and their revolting sexual habits are more than any reasonable man can put up with.'

Only a day or two after saying this we saw something that illustrated the truth of his statement.

Only a few steps from the farmhouse was a glade. There a delicate but infuriated Grant's gazelle was butting with all her might at a full-grown dog baboon which was attacking her newly-born baby. It was a revolting sight. But the impassioned fury of the mother—less than a yard high and delicate in proportion—as she butted with her sharp lyrate horns at the filthy creature's lividly naked buttocks was in the end too much for him. Slavering, and snapping with his long fangs and with his cheek-pouches shaking with aguey frustration he sprang off his victim and turned to deal with the mother; but she, with a lucky upward thrust of her horn managed to pierce his snout. Howling with pain, he bounded off, while the gazelle turned to lick and comfort her baby.

'Filthy things,' Cullen commented.

He then went on to tell me of his latest method of dealing with them; and it was this method I used when called to Kibwezi.

With the help of native labourers I built a big box-shaped frame of bamboo and filled in the sides of the cube with thorn and leaves, leaving interstices just too small to permit the animals' escape. At one end the box had a simple door, hinged at the top and held open by a wire terminating in a catch that would be released as soon as the bait was tampered with.

We used a hand of bananas as bait and went off to watch from behind a screen of thorn bushes.

Not long after six baboons made a raid on the banana bait. Their snatchings released the catch and the door swung down behind them. But undismayed they fought over and ate the bananas.

Then I put the rest of Cullen's plan into action. I made my signal to the nearby house and a crowd of natives armed with heavy forked sticks came running over. Poking their sticks through the cage the natives held the infuriated baboons pinned to the ground. Two or three of the delighted boys held each baboon, forcing both limbs and body to the floor, while another set of boys, whom I had previously armed with some old shearing clippers, entered the cage and clipped various parts of the baboons' anatomy until they looked like patchy motheaten rugs. Then, still holding them at arms' length to avoid the snappings of their long and dangerous fangs, we bedaubed them on every bare patch with brightly coloured paint.

The effect was fantastic. The creatures looked as if they had been smitten with ghastly and contagious diseases, and they were all chattering fearfully as the pungent smell of the oil-paint affected them.

Released, they scampered off with ambling gait, gibbering wildly. We watched them swing immediately to the highest tree tops where the rest of their tribe were roosting. The natives were shrieking with laughter at the grotesque patchwork creatures.

But soon the effectiveness of Cullen's method became

apparent. The tribe in the treetops affected either by colour or smell or perhaps both began to bark with displeasure. It seemed the gaudy ones were not by any means welcome on their return. For a long time we listened to the barks of rejection as the tribe turned against the pariahs. And once or twice, with the aid of binoculars, I saw the painted monkeys sitting dismally examining their patches, scratching and sniffing at the thickly daubed sticky paint and giving vent to their dismay in every possible way.

But it seemed that in the end the tribe accepted them back into the fold with an unexpected *esprit de corps*. They could not, however, face the risk of the mysterious new disease affecting others of their number. They chattered and parleyed about it all that day. Then at sunset the whole tribe decamped, swinging away through the treetops to another region. Eventually, Cullen had theorized, they might forget the incident and return to Kibwezi; but at the very least the estate would be safe from their raids for several months.

Well, I hadn't rid the world of the creatures, but at least I'd despatched them from Kibwezi; and that had been my assignment.

MANHUNT II

THE CACHE

As I looked out across the moonlit plateau and thought of the startled departure of the garish baboons I chuckled mildly. It was a comic recollection, though perhaps it wouldn't have seemed so comic if recalled in broad daylight during a busy day. I suppose I was really clutching at straws in my reminiscent efforts not to become bored with my job of watching and listening. I guess I may also have felt a little resentful towards my present task, too. I like men as companions rather than as hunted creatures. Generally speaking beasts maintain a magnificent dignity when at bay; men so often don't.

However, the tracking down of poachers is a job that has to be done. I decided to try and be a bit more constructive in the use of my time than simply spending it watching and listening and reminiscing. In any case I needed to stretch my legs.

I got down from the truck and took a turn as far as the carcass of the baboon. During the last hour or so a murmuring wind had shifted the arid surface of the plateau once more and our tracks, made earlier in the day, were now obscured. Even as I stood there my immediate footprints were being obliterated as the weightless grains of dust shifted under the pressure of a breeze which would scarcely have dried a moistened finger. And at the same time an even stranger thing was happening: other sets of tracks were being revealed. Even as I watched the dust blew softly away and signs of recent disturbance by digging, as well as feet, could be seen. Evidently the carcass of the baboon had been left there as a sign. And a sign implied the necessity of finding the spot again. Clearly I had by chance discovered the cache we were seeking.

Hurriedly I woke Hardy and we began our excavations.

After only fifteen minutes' digging our spades struck something solid. From then on we went very carefully, scrabbling away at the sandy dust with our fingers.

It was the cache all right. By morning we had laid bare as nice a store of poached ivory as I had ever seen—all of it hidden away in a hole some fifteen feet across and as many feet deep. There were no tusks of outstanding size or quality—30- and 40-pounders predominated—but, pound for pound, the store was worth a nice little sum. And not only was it effectively hidden from sight: it was also safely preserved. Covered by sand or soft earth it is preserved indefinitely from the sun and air.

'What now?'

Hardy and I looked at each other. By solving one problem we'd created another. We had the cache but we were no nearer finding the culprits. And now, in addition, we had to guard or remove a couple of tons of ivory. For I had no doubt that news of our discovery had already reached the bazaars of Kitui. The natives of the village a mile or so behind us would long ago have sent a runner to warn the headquarters of the ivory-buyers' organization. We had been watched since our arrival and we were still being watched.

I write of 'the headquarters of the organization' as if it were some world-flung business with a concrete and glass office in Berkeley Square, or an international spy system. Actually it would be the cunning brain of a little Indian storekeeper named Rammal or Singh gliding with bland obsequiousness among the pots and pans, carpets, sacks and hanging lanterns of his store. Already I could hear his evasions and denials, his shocked protestations of innocence. I'd heard them all so often before. The Indians of East Africa have a complete understanding of both eastern and western standards of morality and are adept at playing one off against the other with infinite advantages to their personal incomes.

It wouldn't be easy to link up the evidence. But at least we'd made a start. Handsore already with our digging efforts we now had to load the ivory into the truck. This we did. By then it was mid morning. We filled in the hole—the shifting sands of the plateau were helpful in doing half our filling for us—and replaced the carcass of the baboon. We were pretty certain that our nocturnal activity had been observed; but that probably wouldn't prevent the poachers coming to investigate. With complete disingenuousness they would no doubt pretend to some activity not even remotely connected with ivory. But at least we were sure they'd come sooner or later; and when they came we'd be ready for them.

'A night to remember,' Hardy said with an edge of sarcasm. It was the very phrase I'd used in telling him a story on our journey out here; and he was mocking me good-humouredly by underlining the contrast between the overt excitement of that night and the furtive discoveries of this one.

A NIGHT TO REMEMBER

THE telegram was marked 'priority' and read *Elephants troubling me please come now. Sands.*

Ken Sands and his wife Anetta had settled at the Sultan Hamud Ranch several years before. They are the likeable and reliable sort who never cry wolf unnecessarily and are normally quite capable of looking after even big-scale troubles, so I knew they had real need of assistance.

I packed a lorry with suitable arms and equipment, chose the native personnel I could most rely on, and left immediately. A few hours later we were encamped at the ranch and Sands was showing me round the estate and pointing out the damage in a silence that was far more eloquent than words. What had once been a flourishing vegetable garden was now a trampled waste: as far as the sight could reach the desolation of uprooted shrubs, trampled seedlings and flattened plantains met the eye. The restocking and nurturing of these acres would take months. Ken and Anetta were not the type to shirk such a heartless task: but clearly there was no point in replanting their gardens until the marauding elephants had been dealt with.

As we walked round the razed fields I saw that the imprints of the elephants' feet were of all sizes: small and large alike had trampled through the fields in search of their objective.

Water.

Conditions of intense drought prevailed at that time. And the Sultan Hamud Ranch offered the beasts the water that had failed at their usual water-holes. They would naturally take the line of least resistance to the next available source; and that happened to be Sands' pumped reservoir supply.

The power plant, which extracted a steady flow from a bore-hole, was housed in a small brick house with a cor-rugated iron roof standing beside a series of large open-topped reservoirs. Thirty or more elephants leaning and pressing against it as they jostled each other while they drank at the reservoirs had done the place no good at all. The bricks had been rubbed smooth by the elephants' bodies and the whole place had a distinct list.

It wouldn't stand many more elephantine leanings. Sands' S.O.S. had been fully justified.

During the afternoon he drove me round the estate in an effort to find out where the beasts lay up during the daytime. There were bulls, cows and young among their number, and I have often confirmed that when there are young to consider elephants have an intense dislike for semi-open bush land, such as this was, where they are most vulnerable to attack. They prefer the tangled thicket. The spoor proved plainly enough that they crossed the single-track railway to make the nocturnal raids on the reservoir and returned before crack of dawn; but I didn't want to pursue them to their day-time home for I knew I'd have a much better chance of dealing with them while they were concentrated at the reservoir.

Accompanied by native bearers we followed the spoor to and across the railway track. I concluded there were about thirty beasts all told; and although the track was heavily metalled with crushed stone not a single piece of this ballast was displaced. Elephants are far less clumsy than rhinos when crossing railways. They have an innate caution which causes them to group together fifty or so yards before they come to the track, pause, listen intently and think the matter over. When they are quite certain no train is approaching the leader will turn and signal to them and they will cross the track in an orderly manner without disturbing even the smallest stone on the bal-lasted track. In contrast to their intelligence in coping with man-made problems like railways one might in-stance the clumsiness of rhinos, which cross the tracks in a wild rush, scattering the ballast far and wide, and the stupidity of giraffes which frequently run foul of trains, bewildered at night by the headlights and in daytime by the approaching roar, and turn to face the onslaught rather than flee.

Having got some idea of the number of elephants I had

to cope with, and their likely line of approach, we returned and established camp fifty yards from the power house and reservoirs.

Sands told me the marauders came only on alternate nights. This was because they were diffident about approaching man-made water supplies even in the desperation the drought imposed upon them.

My plans included of necessity some kind of lighting, for there was no moon. We rigged up a spotlight on the lorry and installed one of the natives behind it so that he could focus the beam as required. There wasn't much else we could do except watch and wait.

During the first night's vigil no elephants came. For many hours no sound but the distant *yoo-e-hoo* of wailing hyenas could be heard. Then suddenly, quite near at hand, an unexpected scuffle broke out. Even before the sounds of the scuffle were heard a revolting stink permeated the air. When Nganda, my rifle bearer, shone his pocket torch we saw with a delight somewhat diminished by the foetid air, that it was a honey badger.

These little creatures of the weasel family—properly called ratels—are, for their size and weight, the most courageous of African animals. They are small, tough-skinned and conspicuously marked. No need for them to be able to camouflage themselves: like skunks they can discharge a smelly fluid at will and this tends to discourage all attackers. But they themselves will attack almost any reasonably sized creature, including the porcupine, whose formidable quills are not always capable of penetrating the ratel's tough hide; and it has been known for them to attack a man who has foolishly and belligerently chosen to ward one off with a stick. In such cases they close immediately with their opponent and attack the legs with upward thrusts of the snout, peeling the skin painfully away.

As their name implies, honey badgers feed on wild-bees' honey; and this one we now saw in the glare of the spotlight was already shinning up a tree towards the nest in a hollowed-out branch near the top. It stopped and turned immediately to face this attack by light. The small ears on its white-topped head were flattened and its weasel teeth already bared. I have never seen so much ferocity concentrated into one small creature. Its tiny eyes were glittering with fearless hostility; and I'm sure that if any of us had made a move towards it it would have taken on the lot of us without a moment's hesitation; for even the blinding light of the torch seemed only to increase its courage and determination.

However, as we made no move to interfere with it—I was in fact far more interested in observing this rarely seen nocturnal creature at work than in doing it any harm—it presently went on its way, clambering skilfully up the tree, and once again the stink permeated the atmosphere. In their pursuit of honey the ratels' method is to asphyxiate the bees in their nest by ejection of the anal fluid, and then to gorge themselves without interruption.

When after some time we saw him emerge—completely ignoring us and the light this time, from which I inferred he considered us quite beneath contempt—he scuttled down the tree with the rapidity of a squirrel and went off into the undergrowth uttering the short and rather charming chortling sounds that always conclude such rampageous expeditions and which to some extent compensate for the nauseating stench and frightening belligerence.

The honey badger offered us our only entertainment that night; but the following night we had rather more to occupy our time.

At 1.15 a.m. we heard the distant sound of the herd's approach. Elephants tread lightly and it was not a reverberating thunder of great feet that we heard: rather, a stealthy sound of herded bodies and swishing foliage as they came on across the railway track and through the fields.

Once again it was a pitch black night. We had installed ourselves fifty or so yards from the power house on the down wind side so that the elephants wouldn't suspect our presence too soon, and we waited a good five minutes after I was certain the herd had reached the reservoir— there could be no doubt about their presence there, for the sound of water being sucked from the reservoirs was unmistakable.

I gave the signal and Sands moved the lorry slowly forward. The native spotlight operator was safely behind his apparatus waiting for my low whistle. Nganda and I went forward step by step.

At about twenty yards I gave the spotlight operator the whistle. The light came on immediately—somewhat to my surprise, for at rehearsals during the afternoon the native had proved a bit slow in responding.

The brilliant beam clove through the darkness. It disclosed a churning mass of bodies round the reservoirs. The tanks were already nearly empty and I could hear the metallic clank of tusks against the metal as the elephants dipped lower and lower.

Scarcely before the jammed herd had time to be surprised by the blinding light I drew a bead on a large beast. At that moment the light went out, and the stygian blackness and the beginning of panic surrounded us. I caught a glimpse of the native behind the spotlight. The sight of the elephants had been too much for him. With an abortive effort at doing his duty he switched the spotlight on again, but in his panic he tipped it to point skyward. With a wild gesture of despair he fled.

Nganda was made of sterner stuff. He has been trained by me in close-quarter shooting methods and has nerves of iron and superb sight.

Weighing up the situation with miraculous speed he rushed past me through the darkness back to my tent. Sounds of anger and panic were increasing among the elephants, but so far they were not concentrated. The surprising light had come and gone too quickly; they were uncertain yet what they had to contend with. In a few seconds Nganda was back: he had grasped not only the situation but the solution too and had remembered that I kept a couple of three-cell hand torches in the tent. One of these he now handed to Sands and one he kept himself. Throughout the ensuing action these torches were our only source of light.

Nganda switched his beam straight into the face of a large lanky bull. Almost instantly I shot it dead—it slid smoothly to earth against the side of the power house. I distinctly heard the iron roof creak with strain.

Immediately behind the dead beast another bull loomed round the edge of the building. This one I shot through the heart. It flung its trunk skyward at the moment of death and a gushing fountain of blood spattered the milling herd.

The scent of blood and death and the crack of my rifle now impelled the concentration of their hate and fear. Terrified and angry the beasts clambered out of and around the reservoirs. They shrieked and trumpeted in death and panic and the sounds of their fear were taken up by the cattle in the corral.

In the midst of this turmoil, with the wavering torch beams our sole illumination, I managed to drop two more beasts. The confusion was indescribable. But it was clear that the herd had decided to scatter. The whole lot were trying to get out at once. But one huge bull, intent on malicious retaliation, decided to charge the power house. I saw him concentrate his enormous strength in one great sideways heave against the wall of the already weakened building. The power house wall collapsed in a thunderous clatter. With a single brain shot the bull fell to its knees and a final upward thrust of its head penetrated the iron roof with its tusks as if the metal had been so much paper.

The herd was fleeing now. In the thin light the bodies passed, sideways on to me and moving too fast now to take an aim. The ground trembled and dust rose in clouds. The last to depart was a cow elephant accompanied by a baby. The little one could not move fast enough and the mother knelt down and scooped her offspring up on her tusks—I could scarcely believe my eyes when I saw this happen, for it is a very rare occurrence and in my opinion is resorted to only in the face of the most dire distress, and then only with babies less than a week old.

When the ground was still again and the last sound of the frustrated elephants' departure had faded to silence we packed up. The ordeal had not been without risk, for the maddened beasts might easily have decided to attack us rather than run. But all had turned out well and now they were on the run—back to Masailand and in search of new water-holes and streams. They would not bother Sands again.

In the morning we saw the extent of the gory desolation. The power house engine and reservoir piping were brightly splashed with the blood of the bull that still lay in the midst of the havoc he had wrought. He was a fine beast, magnificent in anger, and I couldn't help wondering if he was perhaps the sire of the baby I had seen carried to safety by the cow who at great personal risk had knelt down and given me an opportunity to shoot. Thinking now of her bravery and of the immense dignity with which she had rescued her calf, I was glad I had let her go. She, perhaps more than the excitement and danger, made the night a memorable one.

MANHUNT III

THE MERCHANT

EVERYONE in the village was bristling with politeness next morning, so we knew our discovery had been detected. We drove the International back to Hardy's home and left the ivory there where it would be safe. Then we returned to watch.

Hardy, armed with the power of authority of the District Officer, went into the village to try and collect some information. After some time he returned with a native who smilingly explained away the buried ivory by telling us that this was one of the famed elephants' burial grounds. It is a popular superstition that elephants, having lived their allotted span of years, gather at a certain place and will themselves to die. I think romantically inclined writers have done a lot to perpetuate this legend; but I have yet to come within a hundred miles of believing it—or of finding the slightest shred of evidence to support it. So we were unlikely to fall for this ingenuous explanation.

'Yes?' Hardy said with heavy irony.

'No?' The native echoed the irony, widened his smile and went on to assure us that the cache we had found was in fact only a small percentage of the total ivory concealed in this 'elephants' dying ground'.

The curious thing was, that in spite of our disbelief of the legend we could almost imagine that in this dry and lonely place death could be summoned. I remembered the resentful audience of buffaloes drawing ominously nearer on the day we'd arrived. The legend sometimes

21

developed the idea of a congregation of witnessing beasts. Perhaps after all . . .

But that was as near as I ever came to believing the legend of the elephants' burial ground. As I've said, I'm not an imaginative man.

'More?' Hardy said, and shrugged his shoulders. More information sometimes comes when one doesn't appear too interested. Suddenly he switched to another line of approach. 'Tell me the names of the Indians who visit the village. Where do they come from? Voo?'

The native shook his head. 'No Indians.'

'You know you can be fined many goats for poaching —perhaps even jail?—You can also be fined some goats for concealing information.'

The native laughed with happy scorn at such an idea. Concealing information indeed! Hadn't he already explained that this was the elephants' vast dying ground? He went on to add that the natives of the village had some kind of guardianship over the plateau on the elephants' behalf; and from this we inferred that our departure would be welcomed by the spirits of countless generations of dead tuskers.

We did in fact depart: but only to the nearby Indian settlement of Voo. This shanty-town was simply a conglomeration of shacks built round and belonging to the central store, the whole place run by a smiling Indian merchant called Rammal. He welcomed us effusively and gave us the freedom to look around and choose whatever it was we might be wanting. The low ceiling of the store was strung with wire lines from which were suspended a multitude of jangling and clattering wares— tools, boots, saris, pots, gewgaw ornaments from Birmingham, packets of Post Toasties bundled into a fishing net, walking sticks, canned salmon stacked in birdcages, rakes, rolls of muslin—there was an endless and curious variety. And on the floor were stacked more goods—

books, patent medicines, potatoes, flour, razor blades, crates of soda water—so tightly that one shouldered ill-balanced edifices of boxes with alarming results. From time to time things fell down, burst open, spread in liquid or powdery messes across the floor. But Rammal contemplated the disorder with complete equanimity. He made resigned gestures with his hands, tinkled a small handbell and, when three or more of his young assistants came running in merely turned away and let them get on with the cleaning up. This, in spite of immense activity on the part of the assistants, would result in little more than the sweeping back into the packet of some corn-flakes, or the use of some sheets of blotting paper to mop up some spilt paraffin. An easy chaos was Rammal's stock-in-trade. The retail side of his business flourished largely because of the rich confusion of the store, which his white customers regarded as a target for their funny remarks and the natives supposed—mistakenly—to be reflective of the splendid profusion of his wisdom.

Rammal was wise all right; but his wisdom was restricted to the successful conduct of a number of enterprises which needed little more than secrecy and the organization of an elementary intelligence system in which his informers were never quite sure to what extent there was double-crossing going on.

All this we learned in due course. At the time of our first visit there was nothing to do but question him.

'There's some ivory poaching going on, Rammal. Know anything about it?'

'Me, *sahib*?' There was a look of incredulous horror on his face. 'I am injured, *sahib*, that you should think me so unworthy as to indulge in such wicked going-on. I have been here in Voo many years'—and he began a long rig-marole about his arrival in Africa and the building up of his business on principles of honesty and value, of his respect and honour, of his love of elephants and his com-

plete disregard for the value of money. He concluded by
offering to take us into every one of the shacks and out-
houses, or, better still, to let us investigate everything
unaccompanied. 'Go where you will, *sahib*. You will find
nothing—nothing.'

'I don't doubt that,' Hardy said. Nevertheless we did
investigate—thoroughly. We were quite ready to call any
bluff he might be pulling. There was nothing to be found.
If Rammal was indeed the king pin in the poachers'
organization his intelligence service had evidently given
him ample warning of our discovery and investigation.

As we were going away, satisfied in our own minds
that Rammal was our man but quite unable to produce
any evidence that would stand up in a court of law, one
of the young Indians employed by Rammal stepped unexpectedly out from behind a rusty old tin shed where
sacks were stored. 'Watch. Tuesday the *dhow* goes from
Mombasa,' he said.

There was no apparent reason why he should have
given us this information. It was either false, a plant to
deceive us and distract our attention from something that
would be going on in another part of the forest, so to
speak, or else the Indian bore his master a grudge.

We had no time to find out, for he disappeared as suddenly as he had come and we were forced to return to the
village unenlightened. But if the information had a grain
of truth in it it meant that the merchant would have to
get his poached ivory down to Mombasa in three days'
time—a 200-mile train journey. It also meant that he
would either have to recover the ivory we had safely
stored at Hardy's home or lay his hands on more—the
'more' being perhaps the still undiscovered store somewhere in the 'elephants' dying ground'.

We had a problem on our hands, but we decided to
tackle it as best we could.

'Anyway,' Hardy said comfortingly, 'if they act they've got to act pretty soon to get the stuff on Monday's train to Mombasa. It's Friday now.'

If they acted, yes; but the bit of information we'd gathered was more than likely intended as a decoy. The cunning of human quarry is very tiresome when one is accustomed to the straightforward thinking of animals.

THE LIFE AND DEATH OF CHARLES COTTAR

PERHAPS I seem to protest overmuch about the straightforward thinking, the lack of guile, of African beasts. If I do, I must give balance to my protestations by saying something about leopards—in my opinion the most subtle and cunning animals I have come across. This will give me an opportunity to introduce Charles Cottar—a giant among men in both stature and fearlessness.

Many years ago there came to Kenya—then known as East Africa—a man from Oklahoma. He had been a sheriff in the corn belt of that tough state and had acquired a lightning precision as a revolver shot in numerous saloon battles. The sheriff's job and the corn business had bred in him an absolutely simple approach to life. He either liked people or he didn't; and if he didn't, then right was might. His reach was long and his knuckles were hard. He always carried a cudgel which reminded me of the one carried by the giant in *Jack the Giant Killer*, and anyone who upset him would as likely as not get a crack on the cranium. For this reason he inspired fear in many men—particularly as he was a law unto himself and thought very poorly of the man-made rules of social intercourse if they happened to cut across his current wishes.

Cottar was a good six feet four inches tall and invariably wore a loose pair of khaki slacks suspended by strips of red rubber inner tube discarded from Perishing Percy, the Model T Ford that belonged to him and his family. His huge arms and legs bore the scars of many maulings from lions and leopards and his great knuckles stood out like the knobs that protect crocodiles' eyes. I can see and hear him now as he strode with his cudgel down to the post office at Parklands, the small Nairobi suburb where he lived with his six beautiful daughters (they must have taken after their mother) and two of his sons, Bud and Mike. The family had established a fine business as outfitters and guides to *safari* visitors, and many of these appointments and contracts were conducted by telegraph. Woe betide any clerk or civil servant who upset him. He was quite likely to crown with a wastepaper basket any one of them who tried to explain some incomprehensible rule of the administration, and his usual reply to official letters demanding immediate answers was *Sir: Your letter has been before me, it is now behind me. Yours, Chas. Cottar Esquire.*

Naturally this kind of thing didn't endear him to the authorities, and many times he was served with summonses compelling him to attend some particular court on a particular day. These made him absolutely livid, and I easily believed him when he told me he'd dealt with the bearers of two of them—'Two damned blisters, Jock'—by using his rifle.

This great white hunter of the breed so typical in earlier days three times fought single-handed in close combat with leopards.

He hated these beautiful but savage creatures— 'They're so damned nimble, Jock, and their claws like bloody razors'—but of course his clients always wanted

to bag one for the sake of the pelt, and because of his con-
scientiousness as a hunter Cottar would always try to bait
one of the forest leopards; these are much larger and
more beautifully marked than the beasts that roam the
plains and semi-bush land.

On the first of these *vis-à-vis* tussles Cottar had been
lucky in securing for his bait a domestic dog that had died
during the night. Dog flesh is irresistible to leopards and
unscrupulous poachers have even been known to use a
live dog in a box trap as a bait—a device which, along
with that obnoxious engine of pain the gin trap, no
hunter worth the name would ever be guilty of using.
But the fortuitously dead dog was too good a chance to
miss and Cottar strung it from the low branch of a tree
and prepared to await results.

Unfortunately it was one of the smaller, palely marked
leopards that got wind of the bait first and came padding
out of a nearby thicket. But, as if suspicious that such a
desirable meal might mean danger, it skirted the bait
first, keeping closely to the cover of thorn and brush
which, in conjunction with the dappling sunlight and
the beast's rosette markings, made it practically invisible.

And suddenly in its circuit it was down-wind of
Charles, and, still offering an uncertain target by virtue
of its camouflage, was about to spring. But Cottar,
annoyed that this wasn't the leopard he wanted anyway,
made a surprise move himself. Instead of firing he side-
stepped and grabbed the leopard's hind legs as it landed
where he himself had crouched a split second earlier.

Snarling and spitting, the leopard closed with him;
but Cottar's great strength and the long reach of his
powerful arms were too much. With blood streaming
down his arms from lacerations made by the long, poison-
laden claws, Cottar found the beast's throat and wind-
pipe. The powerfully sprung hind legs continued to rip

at him as man and beast tussled on the ground; but after a moment the pressure of those great hands was too much. The leopard died there of strangulation, its long fangs bared and the blood of its killer dripping down on to its belly.

Without further ado Cottar had his wounds roughly bound up and lay in wait for the next victim. Fortunately this was a beautifully marked forest beast which went for the bait without hesitation and which Cottar killed with a single shot. It meant nothing to him that only half an hour before he had been at grips with the other beast; he would no more have thought of retiring to recoup his energies than of flying.

Only a few days after this encounter Cottar was tracking through the bush when he was ambushed and attacked—almost as if in revenge—by two small leopards which sprang upon him from well-camouflaged positions in the trees.

There was no time for warning or preparation. The angry cats were upon him simultaneously, ripping at his body. He flung his rifle to the ground, realizing its uselessness. His towering body proved less immediately vulnerable than the animals had expected. Momentarily loosened from their tenacious grip by his split-second reaction to the attack they found themselves sprawling in a spitting, clawing skirmish at his feet. In that instant of advantage he seized one of the leopards by the throat. His enormous hand encircled its neck with such pressure that the leopard's eyes were suffused with blood. His own blood was running down his arm and colouring the long fangs as it ran into the snarling mouth.

The other leopard, regaining its feet, immediately sprang on Cottar's back; but in doing so it sealed its own death-warrant, for Cottar was already bent forward in his stranglehold engagement with its mate and in ducking a little more the new attacker overshot its leap and landed atop the first beast's kicking hind legs, which immediately ripped its belly.

Cottar took instantaneous advantage of the enemy's misjudgement. He now had both beasts by the throat in stranglehold grips. Their powerful springlike limbs were of course impossible to control and they had forced Cottar to an upright position again. But his grip on the two leopards remained undiminished.

Streaming with blood from the lacerations on his shoulders and arms he now found a new strength that one would have thought even his great body incapable of.

He began to beat the heads of the two leopards together.

The beasts of course gave no quarter. Their lithe bodies threshed air, ground and enemy alike. The group—towering man and grappling leopards—would have been a joy to any sculptor whose inner apprehension could have grasped its power. Cottar's great arms and legs, shredded now with bloody tatters of clothing, seemed endowed with limitless strength. The choking coughs of the leopards, the impact of their skulls, the hissing and lashing of their limbs and tails and Cottar's gasps and splutterings all compounded to make the battle terrible in sound and fury.

All told, two minutes might have passed: scarcely more. Though to Cottar it doubtless seemed like a week. The native bearers, momentarily terrified into beating a hasty retreat when the leopards attacked Cottar, had now edged forward a little, their eyes popping from their heads in wonder and terror at the unique battle. No one could help: a bullet would certainly have gone wide or hit Cottar instead of one of the leopards. Only endurance and sheer strength counted. And it was Cottar's endurance and strength that proved the greater.

Quite suddenly it was apparent that the flailing of the leopards' limbs and tails was flagging in intensity. Cottar grunted joyfully. The grass was slippery with blood from his own wounds and from the ripped leopard's belly. He continued to hold the animals at arms' length and beat their heads together and against the trunk of a tree: the thuds of contact were really quite sickening.

But no more effort was necessary. Strangled and beaten to death in fair and open battle the bodies of the sinuously beautiful beasts now collapsed with Cottar atop of them—still finding immense reserves of strength to beat and squeeze the remaining breath of life from them.

Then he stood up. The leopards lay in the final twitchings of death on the ground. One would have thought that now at least he would retreat and rest; but being Cottar he did nothing of the sort. When his wounds were bound he continued the *safari*.

'Nimble bastards, leopards,' he said. 'Cunning, too, lying in wait like that. Claws like bloody razors.'

This great man was attacked on one other occasion— but this time by a single leopard; and he was able to fend it off with his rifle and shoot it at point blank range. Although mauled about the face and head he suffered little damage to his seemingly inviolable flesh and bone: there were just a few more scars to be seen.

Cottar's death had a sad irony about it.

He had accepted a challenge from those who disliked, feared and shunned him and had engaged to get close-up ciné shots of a rhinoceros. This was in days before the ciné camera had reached its present stage of development and viewfinders were deceptive.

The rhino and Cottar had sighted each other and the rhino—ever a beast of doubtful temper—had decided to charge. A wonderful opportunity: Cottar immediately dropped to one knee and began filming the rhino thundering towards him. But the deceptiveness of the viewfinder was his undoing: he allowed the rhino to come too near—thinking it to be still some way off as viewed through the glass—before taking up his rifle. He managed to fire his shot but the beast's horn had already gored him.

Cottar fell forward without a murmur. Never in his life had he turned his back on an attacking beast—whatever it might be—and this occasion was no exception: the rhino lay a few feet from him, his bullet having found its brain a second too late.

Cottar's death happened many years ago. But although the names of men echo for a shorter time in Africa than elsewhere, many of the native chiefs ask me even today where the great white hunter has gone.

Both Cottar's sons were brought up in the tradition of close fighting with wild beasts—and indeed Mike and Bud became great professional hunters whom I knew and admired immensely. Mike, like his father, had a boisterous sense of humour. On those occasions on *safari* when, as sometimes happens, time drags because of the absence of beasts, Mike often aroused some excitement and no little apprehension by his trick of imitating lion roars and grunts with the aid of a petrol can. Some of the more tenderly innocent visitors quaked in fear in their tents at these lifelike noises, and Bud would invariably accompany them with bogus lion pad imprints made outside the tents of the quaking ones by impressing the knuckles and heel of the hand in the soft ground.

When they discovered the trick that had been played on them the visitors accepted the deception in good spirit not without a tinge of gratitude. But I have a notion that Bud, like all professional hunters of the first class, held such uninitiated innocents in mild contempt and quite shamelessly looked upon them mainly as money spinners.

Like his father he also had a contempt for law and order and some time after Charles's death told me with wry satisfaction that on that very day a summons for some technical offence against the administration had

been awaiting Charles after the movie hunt from which
he did not return.

Since the time of the Cottars leopards have become
sadly depleted in numbers. Fashion created a demand
for the hides and I can remember the days when thousands of them found a ready sale at the coastal towns
when incoming and outgoing ships made port. Perhaps
leopards were doomed from those same days, for they
were surrounded by enemies of many races, all lusting
for the money that could be made by the fortuitous de-
mands of *couturiers* and shoemakers. No longer, nowadays, are leopard pelts to be found at fifteen rupees apiece
in every Indian *duka* from Nairobi to Mombasa.

The use of bow-and-arrow traps is largely responsible
for their elimination. Several native tribes became skilful
in the use of these traps. The traps, which were of the
simplest construction mechanically, were usually placed
by the side of game trails leading to water. A trip cord
spanned the track and when fouled released the bow
string. If the poison on the arrow was fresh immediate
death resulted—for the poison has a paralysing effect on
entering the bloodstream at any part of the anatomy. If
on the other hand a delay had occurred and the poison
became baked dry by the sun, then the effects were not
immediate.

Curiously, this vegetable poison has no effect on the
flesh as meat. I have myself eaten the flesh of a Lesser
Kudu antelope which fell victim to an arrow trap and
certainly experienced no harmful results. The natives
relished the meat even where the arrow had pierced.

In the days when leopards were a power to be reckoned
with their main food was baboon. With the gradual
extinction of this savage but beautiful creature the
baboon population has increased alarmingly. Of course
the baboon becomes in its turn a target for the hunter's
bullets; but there is little æsthetic satisfaction in despatch-

ing these revolting beasts: it is simply a matter of controlling their marauding habits which threaten the farms of European and African alike.

An alarming experience with a very large leopard befell a friend of mine who managed a large timber concern in one of the forested areas of Kenya. Fortunately George had a sense of humour which he could direct against himself as well as against others.

On the morning before his experience with the leopard he had played a prank on two of the workmen at the sawmill. They used a forest lavatory which was simply a platform seat across a stream. George had sawn halfway through the uprights supporting the platform and he watched in high glee the commotion that arose when the workmen, all unsuspecting, put their weight on the seat and toppled forward into the unsavoury stream beneath.

Later that day George attended to a more urgent matter. For some time leopards had been attacking the domestic stock belonging to forest dwellers and the time had come to take more effective steps than the occasional pursuit of a single beast. He had ample timber and had his workmen make him several roomy cages with simple trapdoors held open by a string attached to the bait in the cage. As soon as the leopard entered the cage and attacked the bait the string was released and the door slid down, trapping the occupant, which could then be cleanly finished off with a rifle.

That night a monster leopard was trapped and the following morning a native servant came running to George—*bwana* must please come at once, the enraged leopard was tearing at the wooden cage in a fierce endeavour to escape.

He went immediately, taking his .22 rifle (always used to avoid bullet damage to the pelt) with him. The leopard was snarling with fury. Great slivers of wood from the cage were lying around and the structure shook dangerously as the monster beast plunged and tore at the bars.

George knelt with his rifle and waited for the animal to present a certain target. But its angry pacings prohibited any such delay. He pressed the trigger just as the snarling creature moved its head and the bullet only grazed the cheek, singeing the fur a little.

Now absolutely maddened, the leopard hurled itself at the doorway in an effort to reach this new tormentor. With a loud splintering the door gave way. The leopard paused an instant then sprang. George ducked and dived into the cage as the infuriated beast leapt over him.

Fortunately the leopard did not turn at once and re-new the attack: if he had it is doubtful whether the shattered door would have withstood his onslaught for very long. As it was, workers from the mill came running at that moment and the beast sped away into the forest. Among them were the two whom George had precipi-tated into the muck. They stood and roared with laughter at the sight of George trapped in his own cage; and in a moment George, a great one for poetic justice, began to laugh too.

As for the leopard—it never reappeared. Several new trap cages were constructed and many other leopards were caught; but that one had gone for ever.

One learns from everything, of course; and what I learned from George's adventure was to ensure that cages I had constructed on my own account were reinforced to withstand the furies of giant beasts. I didn't particularly fancy being caught in the same predicament myself. I mightn't be able to duck so quickly.

In days when I was still a youngster, willingly learning from the first-class chaps, I lived in the same avenue in suburban Nairobi as two great professional hunters, Charles Cottar and Leslie J. Tarlton.

Tarlton was a master of the hunting game, a fine wing shot and equally at home with any calibre rifle. He escorted the late Theodore Roosevelt on his first East African trip—an honour he was as proud of as I was of hearing of his exploits.

I well remember one leopard incident in which Tarlton achieved a capture in an ingenious way.

Two daring leopards made their headquarters in what is now known as Nairobi City Park—terrain offering excellent cover for lurking marauders. From the park they made nightly excursions, terrorizing the house-holders of the Parklands area, for leopards frequently enter houses in their search for domestic dogs. The two leopards hunted singly. Valuable dogs were being killed off, and indeed no dog was safe from attack, for the leopards, with their usual cunning, would quite often enter houses unseen by way of the veranda and nothing would be known till the howls of the dog and the sound of the leopard streaking for the cover of the park disturbed the silence.

By lucky chance—or perhaps a hunter's natural instinct—Tarlton one moonlight night came face to face with one of the pair and in a flash dropped the creature dead with a charge of buckshot. The residents of Parklands were jubilant. But they were well aware that they still had the other one to contend with.

Tarlton's capture was a finely marked forest leopardess and during the operation of skinning her he noticed that she was in season. This made him resolve to put a simple trick to the test. He had the genital organs removed and dragged over the ground from City Park to his own residence on Second Avenue.

This method of enticement was completely successful. The following night the boom of a gun was heard: the male leopard had been shot by Tarlton practically on his own doorstep.

This trait of strong sexual attraction—or perhaps one should call it faithfulness—between leopards may have been one of the forces at work in another leopard incident I well remember.

Two friends (husband and wife), their dog and I were camped out on the high plateau of the Isuria escarpment, which overlooks the great Trans Mara game region.

While sitting round a comforting camp fire during the evening our conversation turned to the subject of marauding leopards. I'd expressed my apprehension as to a possible nocturnal visitor, but my friends had soft-pedalled and reminded me that we had a good watch-dog—and indeed there he was sitting with us enjoying the glow of the embers.

'Leopards are more than partial to dogs,' I reminded them.

'Not this one.'

And indeed as I looked at the huge dog with his fierce look and his brass-studded collar I couldn't help but agree that he'd make a formidable opponent.

However, I was proved right. Towards midnight there was a great commotion in my friends' tent—not from any alarm given by the dog but from the overturning of the table on which a whole array of cosmetics was ranged. A leopard—which I feel sure must have been watching us covertly from a nearby tree during our camp-fire conversation—had taken the dog by surprise. A great fight ensued. My friends could do nothing. Several times a shot was attempted, but the confusion in the small tent was indescribable. It must be quite an ordeal to be confined within the space of a few feet with a brave but horrified dog and a leopard out to kill. As it turned out, however, the leopard was foiled.

Its fangs—long, powered by jaws with a killing grip—fouled the heavy brass studs (actually they were pointed

like nails) on the dog's collar. This prevented him exert-
ing the full killing grip. It also must have hurt him considerably, the studs penetrating his palate. During the
leopard's momentary disadvantage the dog must have
seized his opportunity. No one can tell. By the time I
arrived it was all over—no more than a few seconds'
duration in all—nothing to see but the tail of the leopard
in the erratic light of my torch as he streaked for cover.
There was nothing that could usefully be done that night
—except consider and admire the super cunning of a
creature that could gain access and snatch a victim without opposition by using its senses and its extra-sensory
perception to select the moment when the dog was off its
guard.

The following day I picked up several clues to the
leopard's hideout. Footprints were faintly visible along
the game paths near rocky ledges. At a spot where three
ways converged I arranged a rifle trap, using the remains
of a Chandler's Reed Buck as bait.

That evening brought no luck; but at dinner the
following day we heard the distant rifle go off. My bearer
and I immediately visited the trap. By the light of the
torch we saw a beautifully marked leopard lying dead
beneath the rifle muzzle, its tongue gripped tightly
between the powerful fangs. The carcass was still warm
and my bearer prised the jaw apart. There was no mis-
taking our marauder of the night before last: there were
big bruises on the roof of the mouth.

We inserted a live cartridge in the rifle and re-set the
trip-wire of the dumb killer to the bait—which was
already putrefying.

Again there was an interval until two nights later.
Then we found a fine leopardess caught by the same trap.
I had no doubt in my own mind that she had been
searching for her mate and in reaching the end of the
trail had met her own death.

Though merciless to man and beast alike it seems to me a sad thing that these magnificent felines are facing extinction. The rasping sound of their nocturnal grunts is fading from the African night. Too many races have persecuted them in a general lust for their pelts.

MANHUNT IV

THE BETRAYAL

ON the morning following our visit to Rammal's store and the passing of the dubious information to us so furtively by the native we went back to Makindu— deliberately avoiding another visit to the plateau and the arranging of any kind of guard—and fixed up with the stationmaster there for a special watch to be kept on all trains from now on and a message to be sent us by runner if anything suspicious was seen. Then Hardy gathered a handful of his assistants and we returned to the plateau.

We thought it unlikely that the remainder of the hidden ivory would have been retrieved during our absence; but from information and comments in the village we learned we were wrong. Our principal informant—a trustworthy native—told us that as soon as we had departed a great gang of natives had arrived from Voo and had begun excavations with poles, matchets, dibbles, spades—anything that would clear the soft sand away. They had been delighted with their task and its reward and had plainly been sold completely on the 'elephants' dying ground' idea. Much ivory had been taken away.

'Better than I thought,' Hardy said. 'I thought they'd be a bit more subtle than that. They must know that we'll check on all the trains. They'd have been better to leave the stuff where it was and play a delaying game. Looks as if they're playing right into our hands.'

'It could be that it only looks like that,' I reminded him.

'Could be. Anyway let's pay a visit to Rammal again.

39

Maybe he won't be so keen for us to search all the hovels this time.'

But he was. No amount of conjuration or threats could gain from him anything but a bland smile and a gesture of horror that we could so mistrust him. And once again he offered to conduct us round the shacks or to let us go on our own.

'Nothing to conceal, *sahib.* Not one little thing. You look yourself.'

His eyes rolled upward as if calling on God to witness his honesty and his smile beamed out. Truly our informant must be an evil man. Hadn't we, with all our years of experience, yet drawn the obvious conclusion that the entire native population of Africa consisted of thieves, liars, poachers, swindlers, workers of black magic and ill-wishers? Whereas the Indians, etcetera, etcetera.

We knew only too well what our experience had taught us. We also knew that even if we were to ransack every inch below and above the ground of Voo and in the end unearth the hidden hoard Rammal would swear it was all a plant and be given the benefit of the doubt in court. Our only hope was to catch him redhanded. Since he was never likely to go nearer Makindu than the door of his own store—anyway not until the investigation had blown over—but would get unimportant minions to do the loading and despatching, we didn't stand a lot of chance.

However, Hardy arranged for a couple of his lads to be left in Voo—' to keep an eye on anything that might be visible'—and we began a patrol of the plateau, seeking any information that might be useful. We extended our patrol westward back to Makindu.

The little town—still noteworthy as a big-game centre —boasts a neat array of pleasant bungalows erected 'way back' in days when East African Railways were playing an important part in opening up the area stretching from the coast to the Uganda Protectorate. The bungalows have corrugated iron roofs, and although they were built more than fifty years ago they have withstood all the ravages of the tropical heat—which says much for the standard of material and labour then available.

Indian shops again abound—though the standards of commerce are rather higher than those obtaining at Voo —and they all do a flourishing trade with the residents, supplying grain and haberdashery in great variety.

There is a native hospital sponsored by the government. This is a boon, for the inevitable injuries caused by wild beasts need more than elementary attention. The hospital is managed by a very efficient African dresser named Jacob—a charming and helpful soul ever ready to cope with the ailments of Europeans, Indians or Africans. His task is not an easy one. Gorings by rhinoceroses, poisonings by native arrows, complex childbirths, tranquil deaths, drunken headaches—he is likely to meet all these in a single day and he is very seldom caught out.

Another modern innovation is the aerodrome—perhaps landing strip would be a less pretentious term—and although the landings of aircraft were for a long time a continual source of fascination to the natives the novelty has by now worn off a little. Curiously, though, there is one bit of the airstrip that is irresistible to the natives : the windsock. This fluttering tube of cotton is in continual need of replacement because of its equally continual theft by the more light-fingered of the local yokels—who will climb over barbed wire and penetrate all the other obstacles to entry in order to purloin a yard or two of cloth which they then immediately adapt as shirts or pants. No prevention or cure for this kleptomaniac kink has yet been found.

Although Makindu itself is a quite agreeable place to look at—Kilimanjaro towers magnificently in the southern distance, its sentinel slopes and forbidding peak rising in splendour from the heart of a great continent—

and to be in, there is, as in all African townships, a certain element of low life. Detribalized natives come inland from the coastal areas and apply their cunning to lucrative but sinister methods of earning a living. Characters like Rammal seldom have difficulty in finding undercover assistance.

There is a disagreeable amount of prostitution too— mostly by teenage native girls, whose eyes sparkle with charm and who have no need of the cosmetics they smarm themselves up with. During the day they assume an air of respectability by cultivating catch crops or brewing beer—a good source of revenue.

Brawls occur quite often. I remember an incident not so long ago when I was down at Kibwezi, a few miles south of Makindu. Darkness had fallen and I was sitting enjoying a pipe when I heard a distant scream. I saw my personal servant turn his head quickly—and with a fleeting expression of anguish towards the sound—and when I inquired, 'A woman's cry?' he answered evasively, 'She has put her foot on a cobra perhaps.' But a few minutes later we heard a vehicle start up and travel quickly down the main highway towards Makindu hospital. Later I learned that a young native girl had been hit with a poisoned arrow. In her fight to live she had wrenched the shaft from her side, but she was too late. Her assassin had been repelled in his advances towards her a little earlier and had taken his revenge.

I have known only one instance of a poisoned arrow failing to kill. An old grey-haired native was in Kibwezi jail and I inquired of Tony Keen, the police inspector, what he'd done.

'Trying out his marksmanship,' Tony told me. 'The old fool twanged an arrow at a girl—no malicious intent at all, he just wanted to see whether he could hit her. He did. But the arrow went clean through the flesh of her arm and the poison didn't have time to enter the blood-

stream. They used the usual antidote—human urine—
but there was no comeback anyway as the arrow had
passed through the arm too quickly. All the same he's
committed a crime and he'll have to pay the penalty.'

Makindu is now my home and the centre of my game-
ranging activities, and while Hardy and I were enjoying
a well-earned refresher before continuing our patrol I
reminisced about the days when I first knew the place.

The countryside there has remained quiet and un-
spoiled, and there is still a far greater variety of game
than in many of the other hunting areas. Elephants,
rhino, buffalo, giraffe, eland, oryx, zebra, water-buck,
hartebeest, bush-buck, lesser kudu, impalla, and wart-
hog all abound. Lions, leopards and cheetahs are rarer
but still seen occasionally. The plains and bush are well
watered by the snows of Kilimanjaro and tall peptadenia
trees offer shade and beauty.

It is true that the days of big elephants carrying tusks
of a hundred pounds or more are gone. They no longer
roam across the railway track and cause engine drivers
to pull up and toot their whistles. Nor are the high prices
for ivory still in force. It was this high price that made
small shooting parties worthwhile. Now that elephants
are sadly depleted in numbers and their tusks generally
smaller the *safari* has become a much more expensive
business. But still Makindu is a happy place for the
hunter.

I had an uncle, George Hunter, an eminent surgeon
from Edinburgh, who came out to Makindu years ago to
indulge in a big game hunting expedition for himself and
try to get me to return to Scotland to carry on farming in
the family tradition; but I would have none of it. Africa
had cast its spell.

I'm afraid all I irreverently remember of Uncle George
now is a charming incident that followed his *safari*.

He'd decided during that *safari* that he didn't like

rhinos—they'd caused too many of his native porters to drop their loads and shin up trees. However, all the big game accounted for, he decided to shoot birds for a change and give rhinos the right of way whenever he came across them. All went well until he unexpectedly came upon a drowsy cow rhino with her youngster. Alarmed by this menacing stranger facing them they immediately began to lumber towards him. George, clutching his Dickson 12-bore, turned tail and bolted. The heavy thud of feet came on behind him. He flung himself into a convenient bush and waited, puffing with relief, while the cow and her calf went lumbering by. But alas it was a wait-a-bit thorn, and when Uncle George finally rescued himself from its blandishments he was forced to return to Makindu in a highly inelegant state with his breeches torn and his posterior bare. I had a pleasant private chuckle over this occurrence because Uncle George had always belonged to the upstage branch of the family and was fond of talking to his patients— among whom, he never forgot to inform you, he numbered several members of the nobility—of his Big Game Adventures, doncherknow. I suspect that the episode of his pursuit by the rhino was omitted from his clubroom saga.

Life in Makindu—or anywhere else in Kenya for that matter—doesn't allow much time for idle reminiscence. Hardy and I were soon forced to abandon our rest and go out into the bush to extinguish a small fire.

This one was caused, as so many of them are, by a native using a burning faggot to overpower a nest of wild bees in a tree trunk. The natives seem to learn no care in their foragings for honey and during the dry season their efforts are dangerous and sometimes disastrous.

I remember a great fire that swept through the bush at Kibwezi in 1953 and laid bare some five thousand acres of private land—a sisal estate managed by a good friend of mine, Captain Robert Bennett. There had been a long period of drought and on the day the fire broke out there was a high wind which quickly fanned the flames towards an area where the sisal fields had fallen into disuse and had become entwined with thick masses of thorn and scrub. Monkeys, baboons and many kinds of antelope had their homes there.

Although Bob Bennett quickly mustered all his available labour it was only a matter of a few minutes before the whole of the waste land was alight and threatening the heart of the cultivated area. It was a furnace. Sisal crowns, baked by the heat, exploded and shot off burning faggots like fireworks. The green stems wilted and burned furiously with an explosive roaring. A raging, deafening tide of fire encroached on every living thing. Baobab trees of a hundred years' beautiful growth began to blaze, their blistering bark pouring volumes of smoke to the sky, which was blackened and filled with ash and sparks.

As the day passed the fire extended its dominion over the whole of the farm. The air became so hot and dry that even on quite distant roads car engines began to cough and splutter as carburettors failed through lack of air in the mixture. Natives, Indians and Europeans, blackened alike by flame and smoke, fought their losing battle against the fiery advance. Above the raging flames kites and roller birds wheeled and circled, sensing that their unending appetite for insects might now be assuaged but faced with the great heat into which they would have to plunge. From time to time one of them would be sucked from the sky into the heart of the fire.

Amongst the animals bewilderment and terror reigned. Monkeys and antelopes made frantic attempts to escape. Their screams and chatterings could be heard mingling with the exploding sisal and crackling thorn. But they could not escape for wherever they turned the flames met them. Pythons and other reptiles sought refuge in the uppermost holes and branches of trees; but they were burnt to death as the fire licked upward through the trees.

Gradually the clouds of rolling smoke enveloped the countryside for many miles. At evening the fire still raged. Everyone who turned his thoughts from the immediate business of beating it out could comprehend only desolation and despair. No respite came with the sunset.

Then, in Bob Bennett's household, prayers for relief were offered up. And miraculously, a little while later, the high wind subsided, calmness reigned, clouds banked in the heavens to mingle with the billows of smoke, and torrential rain began to fall.

Next day the charred earth stretched for miles. Hundreds of antelopes' carcasses were strewn over the land, blackly roasted. It was a sad day for Bob Bennett; but for the hundreds of natives it was a day of rejoicing. Antelope meat—already cooked. The bodies were brought in by willing hands, dragged across the ruined land and eaten with sacrificial fervour.

The fire Hardy and I extinguished was of no significance. But it is well to remember that the threat of destruction to life and property is ever present.

We had a brief night's rest and then continued with our patrol. Although it may seem that we had no plans and our movements were aimless, in fact it is seldom possible to formulate any plans when one is dealing with underground goings-on controlled by Indians, or, for the matter of that, native Africans. One is met at all stages by bland denials in the face of incontrovertible evidence, and, when lies fail, a considerable subtlety. Every case has to be built up on information fortuitously acquired as much as on circumstantial evidence, and for that reason much of the case-building consists in watching and listening.

We heard at Makindu station that Tuesday's train would be halted for a considerable time while its load was unhitched. Also, we found a railway employee who for the equivalent in kind of thirty shillings revealed far more information than was visible on the dotted lines of a batch of consignment notes. His betrayal led us to the documentary certainty that the consignor of a load of Benares ware to be loaded at Makindu on Tuesday was a merchant named Rammal.

SERPENTS

ON the whole Kenya is remarkably free from the sinuous threat of snakes. They exist, of course, but nowadays one seldom hears of deaths attributable to snakebite—partly because the Fitzsimmons serum outfit is freely available and partly because many of the more dangerous types are extremely lethargic during the long dry spells common in Equator areas. During the rainy season, though, I am continually alert for the silent threat of the serpent.

Superlatives need careful consideration, but so far as I have been able to establish by my own observation, backed by a certain amount of verification from Nairobi museum, Africa's deadliest snake is the Gaboon Viper (*Bitis Gabonica*), normally found in the forested area west of the Nile in Uganda. This creature grows up to six feet in length and is as great in girth as a man's thigh. Death from its venom comes within two minutes of being bitten. A formidable attacker. I haven't come across it in Kenya, but a Gaboon once attacked a friend of mine, Fred

Pickwell, who is Supervisor of the Post and Telegraph Services in the Colony.

Fred was supervising the construction of a new trunk route in the Mabura Forest and had had some trees felled to make a clearing. In the clearing he was setting up some wooden posts to indicate the course of the trunk line. While driving one of these posts into the ground he heard one of his native workmen cry 'Samama, bwana!' ('Stay put!') In the same instant he realized that a snake had climbed with incredible speed up the post and had touched his forearm and cheek. In the same moment Fred heaved himself backward from the snake's thrust and the native hurled a mallet he fortunately happened to be holding. His aim was accurate and the snake was killed instantly; but it was a nasty moment and appeared even nastier in retrospect when, on examination of the rich red and green autumnal tints of the snake's skin it was found to be a Gaboon.

Of the many kinds of snake in Kenya the cobra and the mamba are the most truculent and the most dangerous. Time and again I have been confronted with cobras—daring creatures which go out looking for trouble and never bother to wait for it to come to them. Their particular trick is to eject their venom into their victims' eyes, and this they can do with deadly accuracy up to a distance of nine feet. I know—I've proved it by protecting my eyes and teasing one with a stick. The second ejection, however, is effective only for about four feet, and the third is a mere trickle of a few drops. The venom is forced from the fang by muscular pressure. After ejection forty-eight hours elapse before a lethal dose of venom is again accumulated. Cobras move very swiftly, their hooded heads raised well up from the ground, gliding through foliage and up trees with sinuous and sinister beauty. They are as treacherous in mood as rhinos and quite often appear friendly towards the owners of chickens and eggs they are attacking. Once gorged, however, they will spit in the eye of anyone who happens to be around.

I know only one instance of the taming of a cobra. A native boy who lives near my home in Makindu catches them and draws their fangs—apparently without much resistance on the part of the snakes, which thenceforward live literally as closely as possible to the boy, for they are always curled round his body with loving affection while he feeds them daintily with porridge. One of those curious cases of animal-human understanding.

Cobras are, in their satanic way, quite fearless. I have often tried to despatch them by running over them with a truck while travelling along the main Makindu–Kibwezi highway. But this seldom succeeds, for they have the ability to hurl themselves from the path of the oncoming truck with incredible speed.

On one occasion, I remember, I was driving at speed down the highway at night, passengers aboard, headlights full on. Suddenly in the swathe of light as I rounded a curve an immense cobra appeared along the dust-track beside the road. It didn't begin to cross the road but instead began to rear up, swaying from side to side as the car approached. In the lights its serpentine writhings gleamed. Then as the truck drew level it leapt from the track and landed on the bonnet. Immediately it began spitting at my passengers and me. The windscreen ran with its venom. I had to alight and shoot it without further ado or it would probably have insinuated its way into the cab.

The biggest cobra I ever saw was shot by Bob Bennett, whose sisal estate at Kibwezi was devastated by fire—a tale I've told in an earlier chapter.

A trader on this estate had heard sounds of laboured breathing in his house. For two days this sound, which resembled human sighing, went on untraced. Eventually the trader looked under his own bed. There on the cement floor lay a cobra curled in U-shape. He bolted from the house. Fortunately Captain Bennett was at that moment motoring past. He ran in and shot the cobra with an ounce of No. 6 from a 12-bore.

Soon after this I arrived on the scene, summoned by Bob to record measurements. The cobra was 12 feet 3 inches long, 10½ inches circumference at the centre, and 8 inches wide at the hood. Never before or since have I seen such a cobra; I believe it may prove a record for all time.

An incident in which my presence proved of more practical value occurred while I was dealing with some depredatory rhinos near Makindu.

I had a dozen or so Wakamba natives to move my *safari* equipment, and when we arrived at my base camp I sent a few porters off to get water. Within half an hour two of them returned—carrying between them the body of a third.

'*Bwana*, he has been bitten by cobra.'

The man was laid in my tent. It was obvious he was in a state of utter collapse and that his condition was grave. Two tiny trickles of blood were oozing from the punctures on his left arm.

Hurriedly I opened the medical box and made ready the Fitzsimmons kit. I tied a tourniquet above the man's elbow, withdrew half the contents of a phial of serum and injected it under the skin above one of the fang punctures. Then I made deep incisions through each wound and rubbed in permanganate crystals. Fifteen minutes later I injected the remaining serum from the phial above the other puncture.

The man's body was limp. I picked up his sound arm and released it: it dropped lifelessly to the ground. In a few minutes he had been brought by the poison to within an inch of death.

For the next forty minutes we spooned warm goat's milk down his throat. He was ashen in colour, there was no sign of recovery at all.

Then suddenly a few milky bubbles gathered at the corners of his mouth and his colour began to change. This change was followed by intense muscular spasms. His neck, arms and legs appeared to be recovering from shrinkage and contraction caused by the poison. It was a great joy to me to see this man recover from what had seemed certain death.

By the following morning he was completely well. Once the effects of the venom were neutralized his splendid natural strength had triumphed. He was profusely grateful to me and told me that now his widowed mother would still have him to look after her.

When I mentioned the incident to Jacob at Makindu Hospital he told me that the timely injections had been the means of saving the man's life. Had I lost time by taking him to hospital the case would without doubt have proved fatal.

There was another case which had a sad ending. This was when I was at Nzui in the Wakamba reserve. Early one morning an old native in great distress came to my tent and begged for assistance. His little daughter—she couldn't have been more than twelve—had been drawing water from a pool when a cobra had attacked her.

I went immediately to her hut. There she lay jerking convulsively and quite clearly at death's door. The snake had bitten her above the ankle and the native mother-cure-all had smeared some quite useless concoction round the punctures. But nothing had been done to stop the poison circulating in the blood, and an hour had elapsed since the little girl had been brought home.

With a hypodermic syringe I injected the Fitzsimmons anti-venom serum, but my common sense told me that no antidote could save her now.

So it proved. A few minutes later she was dead.

The old man bowed his head. In the face of death the Wakamba are always philosophical. 'It is the will of God.'

With this very Christian philosophy go many curious remedies for illnesses and complaints that may not after all be the will of God. Many of them are distillations from tree bark or roots of certain bushes. But the more enlightened natives have now become converted to European lines of thought and use such things as Sloan's Liniment—taken internally!—for chest complaints. Ordinary bluebag intended for bleaching washed clothes is quite often swallowed in the belief that it will cause a miscarriage. This curious insensitivity to pain is manifested in other, more spectacular, ways. I have often seen native men and women have quite horrifying wounds caused by goring sewn up on the spot with ordinary needle and cotton. They never bat an eyelid but watch the proceedings with interest.

Whenever speaking to natives about snakes I always try to convince them that absolutely instantaneous treatment is the only thing.

Whether snakes are poisonous or not they have other natural enemies besides man—for whom they have, of course, a symbolic significance.

Various members of the mongoose family are strongly anti-snake; I have known a fight between a mongoose and a cobra to go on for two hours, with the two creatures indulging in all the finesse of some subtle fencing match. And among birds the secretary bird, which has powerful wings and long legs, is also a snake killer—but on a small scale. I have never seen the secretary attack anything in the cobra or python class.

The ground hornbill, on the other hand, is actually a hunter of snakes and relishes the flesh as food. This curiously ungainly bird with its dead black plumage and white wing markings is now, I am glad to say, protected from indiscriminate killing in Kenya.

On two occasions I have come across ground hornbills attacking cobras. Their method is to stand motionless on guard on the ground for as long as may be necessary if a snake eludes them and goes to earth in a burrow. One of those I observed waited for three hours for a cobra to emerge from a hole in which it had sought refuge. Immediately it was out of the hole the hornbill was upon it. Using its powerful wings and wicked beak it buffeted the cobra against the rocky ground until it died. Then it flew off with the body dangling from its beak, its ungainly flight in no way impeded by the burden. Cobras and other big snakes that never hesitate to rear up against man or vehicle will whenever possible evade the hornbill.

Once, too, I watched a deadly fight between a buzzard and a cobra, and managed to get a picture of what must surely be an unusual combat. The serpent and the bird were locked in deadly embrace for several hours—the cobra's coils wrapped tightly round the buzzard, while the bird's powerful claws had penetrated the snake's skull. Over and over the two rolled, neither would give an ell, and in the end I killed the two of them with smart taps with a heavy tyre lever. But I shall always remember the unremitting fury of the buzzard's attack and the speed with which the cobra responded by flinging its coils round and grappling with the unexpected adversary. I can only suppose the buzzard risked the attack for the sake of food; but it is very unusual for these birds of the vulture family to prey on live snakes of so formidable a character.

The puff adder is very common in Kenya; but it is not truculent like the cobra and its movements are much slower. On the other hand, it can be dangerous underfoot, for one all too easily treads on it when moving through longish grass.

I came unpleasantly close to one of these long-fanged snakes on one occasion when I was following the spoor of elephants in Teita country. I had failed to come up near the elephants, the sun was beginning to set and I thought with no light heart of the many long miles back to camp. To gain a little courage for my journey I lay down to rest beside a grassy anthill.

With my cheek in the palm of my right hand I stretched out and relaxed. Suddenly I heard a hollow hissing noise. Only a few inches from me in a grass-covered run lay the puffer in his nest. Even when I moved some of the protective grass covering the creature did not move and it was quite easy to kill it with a stick. But I was glad I'd heard the hissing before I drifted off to sleep. Now I resumed my rest without further disturbance.

On another occasion I was in the Makueni area of the Ukamba reserve, engaged once more on rhino control work. A heavy shower had fallen, followed by brilliant sunshine. I wandered out of my tent and saw a large snake, earthy green in colour, sliding over the ground a few yards in front of me.

Picking up a stick I followed the slithering creature. When I saw it again a few minutes later among some short grass I gave it a thwack across the middle. Immediately it recoiled and struck towards me, but I managed to get in another blow and this time I killed it.

It was a nice specimen, some nine feet long, and I had it put in a container of spirit and despatched to Nairobi museum. When their letter of acknowledgement came I was amazed to learn that I had sent them a mamba—one of the most deadly of all snakes. Fools rush in! If I'd known at the time that I was facing such a formidable adversary I should never have attempted to do battle with a stick. A gun is really the only answer in such cases. But as so often before I had been lucky.

MANHUNT V

THE CHASE

THE Indian who had betrayed his master for thirty pieces of silver—as we then thought—was a young soft-eyed man called Mr. Karemchoud. He was proud of the 'Mr.' in a subtle way that had nothing to do with vanity. Even the stationmaster used the prefix. Mr. Karemchoud saw it as a privilege that even Englishmen didn't accord one another when they were on friendly terms. Therefore he was lifted above them in some strange way. His mind worked in this upside-down fashion, as we later proved—though indeed the stationmaster told us that he had a curious mental twist that led him always to do things in the most complicated possible way.

'For instance, he never uses long division when working out the *pro rata* cost of some freight charge, but arrives at his solution by an immensely complex series of short division sums. Of course his figures are always accurate nonetheless, and there's plenty of time, so we don't bother him. Besides, his work's extremely neat and looks good in the books.'

'I'm wondering,' Hardy said to me, 'whether he's proved too easy a nut to crack. Would you like to pop back in the truck to Voo and do a bit of detective work there, see if you can dig up any doublecross on this information?'

'You know me. I've not much talent when I come up against human beings. They're too cunning for me. I daresay they find me the same.'

'You're cunning enough in wheedling yourself out of going to Voo,' Hardy said dryly. 'Okay, I'll look after

Voo, you stay around here and watch proceedings. Keep your ears open.'

I said yes I would. But there isn't much to keep your ears open to in the way of conversation in Makindu. It was Sunday and I drove northwest up the railway track to Kiboko.

Kiboko is where Hilda and I plan to live in a year or two's time. Two of my sons are architects and one of them has designed *Hunter's Lodge*, which is now being built by native contractors. There we shall establish a guest house for *safari* visitors and there I shall have my own private game reserve and my own fishing. Electric light, telephone, private water supply, the big old furniture with its fine polish which I have shipped out from Scotland, Africa outside the windows, ourselves inside—there is nothing more to desire. If I get that far it will be extremely pleasant; if not, I have had as much happiness as I need or deserve.

I walked between the walls of the unfinished house. There were no workmen there today and the bricks had a monolithic remoteness—stacks of them leaning a little drunkenly, none of them having yet achieved anything that bricks can become: a home. It was a little sad. But for an instant I saw it all finished, my collection of snuff-boxes stored, the rooms filled with people for whom a *safari* is an adventure—a profitable one maybe, but an adventure anyway, with an æsthetic of its own, like a bullfight.

But at that moment of dreaming a native boy on a bicycle came puffing and clattering down the road, his face shining, his teeth grinning widely. There was something about the rattle of his approach that reminded me that, though I'd promised Hardy I'd keep eyes and ears alert, I wasn't likely to find much that was relevant to our manhunt in the site of my future home. I rather guiltily took the message from the boy.

It was a telegram from Hardy: *King Pins plans more involved than we think. He has disappeared but Mr. K. has arrived. All toing and froing designed to take our interest off something else. What. Any clues your end.*

There weren't; but I couldn't help feeling a bit guilty about not having tried very hard to find any. The position as I saw it was simple. Rammal was the guiding power behind the poaching ring. He knew we'd discovered part of his hoard. He also knew that we knew he'd have to get it to Mombasa on Tuesday's train if he was to fulfil his obligation. So we'd be watching. It was consigned as Benares ware, and by now he probably knew that we knew that too. So perhaps he'd change all his plans; but whatever he changed he couldn't change the date of the consignment. So far as I could see we only had to stop and examine the train. We had the documentary evidence that would convict Rammal.

But it was obvious that Hardy, with his considerable experience, knew that Rammal wasn't going to let us catch him as easily as that.

I put the lad and his bicycle aboard my truck—much to his delight—and we drove back to Makindu. There I telegraphed Hardy: *Nothing doing this end yet but am all eyes and ears.*

A train came in, puffing and blowing just as they had when I first came to Kenya and worked on the building of that very line back in 1910. But nobody got off it except a native farmer with two goats. The driver leaned out of the cab and had a long desultory conversation with a native woman. Then the train began to pull out. It was only as it was gathering speed that I glimpsed a face in one corner of a dim compartment.

Rammal—blandly smiling.

I went back into the telegraph office to wire Hardy about this new development. Obviously Mr. Karemchoud, working along his normal complex system of action, had gone to Voo to warn Rammal. He could quite easily have telegraphed or sent a native bearer (I had my doubts about the existence of a telegraph in Voo), but no—he had to go personally. And now Rammal was escaping.

I wired Hardy that I was in hot pursuit and turned to leave the office: but at that moment the clerk came in from the inner sanctum where the apparatus was. He was flapping a message form at me: 'Priority, sir, *sahib*. Most urgent understand.'

The message was from the District Commissioner: *Most urgent. Man-eating lion creating havoc Darajani. Three native victims. Deal immediately.*

I felt an immediate glow of satisfaction. 'Immediately' meant that I could justifiably desert my rather dreary watching and waiting job and go into action at once. Nothing could have pleased me more. I gave the clerk a hearty handshake of approval—startling him—and rushed to prepare.

Darajani lay about thirty miles down the line. It was not the first time I had been there for the same purpose. Previously I had received a summons of equal urgency when I had been on routine ranging work at Kitui.

On that occasion I drove down from Kitui with all possible haste. A native girl had been dragged by the man-eater from the hut where she slept between two other sleepers. Nobody had awakened. (That didn't surprise me, for natives sleep like the dead and could easily be trampled to death in the midst of an elephant stampede without changing even their rate of breathing.) The only clues to the girl's death were the indications of a body having been dragged through a patch of dried maize stalks and the dismembered arm and leg that lay in the sandy soil surrounding the village.

The whole village, and especially the railway station staff, were living in great fear. No one dared go out after darkness. Terrified natives clung to each other in the dubious safety of their huts after sunset and took it in turns to set up a great clanking of empty petrol cans in an effort to scare the invader away. None of the railway points was manned and the trains were becoming dangerously affected, which could easily result in Nairobi being cut off from Mombasa.

I walked round the little trading settlement trying to weigh up the possibilities of catching the lion.

The place was torrid and waterless. As far as the eye could see there stretched only a tangle of inhospitable thorn and a few stunted trees near the railway. There was no game of any kind in sight; the only living animals were the few gloomy looking sheep and goats owned by the villagers. The water supply was by a single stand pipe, and from this and the trough beneath it the lion had recently slaked its thirst; but the beast's tracks were no indication of its present whereabouts, for they faded out on the hard ground a few hundred yards across the plain.

One thing was clear: the lion was in urgent need of food and was incapacitated in some way, for it is only the physical inability to catch their normal animal food, or the mental quirks that are caused by some long-endured wound, that will induce lions to attack human beings unprovoked.

I decided that the most effective way of catching the lion in this village, where there were approaches from all directions, was by erecting the usual rifle-trap or dumb killer. This simple device consists of two wooden uprights joined by two cross-pieces to which the rifle is tied, muzzle pointing downward. The bait is fixed on the ground between the uprights and the trigger of the rifle is pulled by a wire which passes over a pulley at the top of the frame and down to the ground, where it is fixed. Pressure of the lion's head on the wire as it worries the bait pulls the trigger and the lion shoots itself. These traps are one hundred per cent effective, the animal being shot through the vertebrae at the base of the skull every time.

I fixed up two of these rifle traps and carefully concealed them by building up thorn enclosures all round them. Then arose the problem of baiting the traps. I spent the afternoon and evening looking for some kind of antelope, but a hunt round the arid scrub soon convinced me that no game was likely to be revealed anywhere in the vicinity. I then tried to buy a sheep or goat from one of the villagers, but even in the midst of their terror they proved mercenary and tried to insist that if the lion was caught by using one of their domestic animals as bait the skin of the lion would be their property. I didn't feel disposed to agree to any such condition and told them that I'd look elsewhere for my bait—and that they must take the consequences if the man-eater returned during my absence. I then took my truck and drove off some miles across the plain. Eventually I came across a small herd of hartebeest, shot a couple of them and returned the following day.

The lion had not made another attack. I knew that it would be almost certain to return soon—probably the next day, for it would by now be getting desperate for food again.

I had the hartebeest slit open and dragged round the village to make sure the ground was well scented. Then I fixed one in each of the traps and retired to wait events.

That night I lay dozing in my hut. The night was utterly silent, full of an eerie stillness which in the circumstances was more disturbing than any amount of clatter or animal noises. From time to time I awoke from my uneasy sleep, but no rifle shot sounded. Once a train passed and I heard the stationmaster rush out of his office to hand the driver the token that gave him right of way to the next station. Then he raced back to the office and shut the door. Nothing else happened. I was disappointed.

But I wasn't very far out in my reckoning after all. The following night, in the heart of the sinister stillness, the sound of a shot pierced the silence. There was no other sound—not even a grunt, so I could not be absolutely sure that we had killed the lion. Conceivably it could have been some other creature that had set the trigger off. Anyway it was a pitch dark night and neither I nor the natives felt disposed to take any chances by carrying out an immediate investigation.

But at daybreak we were out. And there under the rifle lay the man-eater of Darajani, a large lioness, stiff and cold.

With native help the lioness was tied between two poles and carried in triumph to the station platform. The villagers gathered, their faces glad with relief, their voices applauding the death of the killer that had stalked among them.

We skinned the beast and it then became clear why she had turned killer. Porcupine quills were deeply embedded in the muscles of her forearms, in her throat, and in the tendons of her hind legs. Handicapped by the pain inflicted by the quills—it must have been similar to that experienced by a man walking with hobnails penetrating his feet—the lioness would be unable to catch her natural prey, zebras. Hence her need to resort to some unresistant creature such as a sleeping human being.

It was evident that there was nothing in her stomach but the remains of a native's scalp; it was equally evident that she was suckling young. Somewhere in a concealed nook or cave amidst the thorn that dotted the rocky plain her cubs lay snuggled, waiting for their mother, who would not now return. I made some effort to find them, but there were no clues to their hideout, and in the end I had to give up the search.

As I drove down to Darajani again, keeping my foot on the pedal and honking like mad every time anything threatened to get in my way, I had the feeling one so often gets of having lived all this before. Only of course, I told myself, I *had* done it before. Hunter to Darajani to catch man-eating lion. The thing was, I knew very well I'd done it before and hadn't the need, as one usually has, to dredge about at the bottom of memory and try to work out if it was all a dream. Except that I was coming from Makindu instead of Kitui the circumstances were exactly similar.

I got to Darajani in something less than an hour after receiving the message. The village lay tranquil under the sun, its gloomy sheep and goats grazing pessimistically on the sparse grass that sprang up from the dusty earth. The torrid plain stretched away into the distance, empty of life. A little train with a couple of wagons sat in the goods siding behind the stationmaster's office. There was no sign of any fear.

The stationmaster came out of his office when he heard me pull up with an heroic screaming of brakes. He looked suspicious and surprised. I told him I'd come to help to catch the man-eater and he looked even more astonished. No man-eater, he assured the *bwana*, had passed their way since that last ferocious beast the *bwana* had relieved them of five, six years ago.

'But——' I began. I looked in my pockets for the telegram and there it was: *Most urgent. Man-eating lion creating havoc Darajani. Three native victims. Deal immediately.*

Then I realized that the message was a verbatim copy of the one I'd had five years previously. It was the similarity of the wording that had irked my memory. Mr. Karemchoud, having access to the filed copies, had

simply chosen that one because of the urgency of its
content and had it passed through the telegraph as a new
message, knowing that I would drop everything for a
priority call from the D.C. Mr. Karemchoud evidently
had reasons for wanting me away from Makindu at this
very moment when I was standing yattering in a village
thirty miles away.

Furious with myself for my stupidity I jumped into the
cab and began my journey back to Makindu. Whatever
it was that was happening there it was probably all over
by now.

In spite of my speed it seemed the longest journey I'd
ever made.

GREAT MEN, GREAT HUNTERS

THE road I sped along crosses and divides Territories of
Kenya which were—and in many respects still are—
among the finest hunting grounds in the world. Masai on
the left, Central on the right, Rift Valley and Nyanza
ahead; and behind me and across the border and beyond
the magnificent slopes of Kilimanjaro the Northern and
Lake Victoria Territories of Tanganyika.

Up to the early 'thirties these provinces of East Africa
were little known geographically and even less known as
hunting grounds. There were over thirty varieties of
game to be found in Masailand alone. In the late afternoon coolness the plains were massed, as far as the eye
could see, with blissfully feeding animals. Groups of
lions, the tiny dik-dik antelope, rhino, elephant. And in
the deep pools below the banks of the Telek watercourse
there were crocodiles waiting to take their toll of the un-

suspecting antelopes which came to drink—monster crocodiles which had drifted down from the Mara Stream, and which could be heard dragging the unwary gazelles below the water to drown before being abandoned to the heat of the sun to rot as a preparation for being eaten.

Westward towards Lake Victoria and south-eastward towards Kilimanjaro the unbelievably magnificent sunsets of Africa spread their brilliant light over a vast natural plain scarcely known by man. Masailand was, and still is, the showpiece of all Kenya. It has become known and hunted; but happily there has been little indiscriminate killing, and Government control is now fiercely resistant to all but necessary and licensed hunting.

Very little migration of animals from Masailand occurs. The altitude is just right—some 5,000 feet above sea level—the plains are well watered, and there is plenty of natural cover. Seasonal migrations are therefore seldom necessary: beasts merely wander from one part of the province to another as the fancy takes them— unless prolonged drought should drive them away.

I remember discovering Masailand in 1930—largely through Denys Finch-Hatton, a son of the Earl of Winchelsea.

Denys, like me, was a professional hunter constantly bothered by the need to find new areas to which we could lead our clients' *safaris*. It is all very well to think of Africa as a great continent and Kenya as a large colony, but there are many other considerations beside apparent size. The richness of the area for game is all-important; also its accessibility and its terrain. Can one get there in a convoy of trucks with all the equipment of the modern hunter? and having got there is the area one in which you can easily continue to transport material by native porter from base camp to outlying camps established daily in the game country? One also has to consider fresh water and game food, for it is of course impossible to carry large quantities of food from camp to camp and the native porters—if not the hunters—tend to sulk if they don't have fresh antelope or other palatable meat each day. Which is reasonable but a nuisance. Distances, stamina and health also need careful consideration. So some kind of compromise is nearly always necessary; and it is the professional hunter's constant problem to find the ideal site so that there shall be good sport and satisfied customers.

Denys and I had long considered Masailand as our next subject for exploration. But we had both been warned by countless native bearers that it was a waterless region and quite impossible for hunting.

However, we made up our minds to have a look, and one day we set out in a Chevrolet truck, accompanied by four natives, to inspect what we hoped would be wonderful lion country in the southern half of Masailand where it borders Tanganyika.

All the field maps available showed nothing but blank spaces; but we decided to strike towards the Mara river across rocks and gullies beyond the black cotton morass of Lake Province.

The going was very difficult and to increase the troubles of our first day's journey the grass was so long that we failed to see a rock which fouled the Chev's oil sump and tore a great rent in it. Denys being mechanically minded, he managed to remove the sump and patch it up: but we had to go very slowly after that both to avoid repeating the damage and to find suitable gaps in the many gullies and sandy drifts. At dusk we reached a rocky eminence and decided to call it a day. We fed and turned in and wondered what the morrow would bring.

During the night we heard the mighty roaring of lions

from every direction. Although dog-tired we could not help discussing the possibilities of this new land of adventure, and at dawn we were on our way again.

For some time we forged ahead very slowly, using tracks which clearly had been trodden by countless hooves of plodding rhinos and elephants. We were deeply grateful for the pioneering spirit and ability of these beasts, for they eased our journey immensely.

After a while the going seemed to get easier. Spoor of many different kinds of animals was much in evidence. We now had even higher hopes for the unfrequented plains beyond, for there was no sign of human life at all, nothing to signify that the tranquillity of wild life had ever been disturbed.

By noon we had overcome all difficulties imposed by the terrain. Rocks, gullies and pitted tracks lay behind us. We had reached the plains of the Southern Masai.

Denys and I could scarcely believe our eyes when we saw the countless beasts ruminating there. Several lions appeared almost immediately, but our presence meant nothing to them, they merely looked at us with mild curiosity and walked away. The abundance of wild life naturally gave each individual creature a sense of security. There were only the hazards of natural victimization to cope with among themselves and they so far had no reason to suppose that we—and our auto—were other than some new species of wild beast. Their reaction was to act as if nothing at all had happened. Lions, buffalo, rhino and antelope of every conceivable variety continued to graze unconcerned. Every slope as far as the eye could see, even through binoculars, swarmed with game.

Flushed with excitement Denys and I began to tour the area immediately. We wanted to prepare a survey of the great plains, giving some idea of concentrations of stock, cover and watercourses. We found that we had been entirely misled as to the supply of water: there were streams and pools galore. We also wanted to get some idea of the quality of the stock. And as the days went by and we toured Masailand mile by mile we discovered that creatures of the finest strains inhabited the area. We saw many elephants with tusks of over a hundred pounds apiece, the lions were invariably magnificently maned specimens, and the zebras were fat and sleek. Natural development through countless undisturbed generations had had its natural result and all was perfection.

Our task of inspection and survey completed, Denys and I now had only to bring our parties of visitors out here and give them some of the finest sport to be found in Africa.

This we did, and between *safaris* we hunted quite a lot together, always exploring new ground and trying—ever unsuccessfully—to get good motion pictures of charging buffalo. Denys pursued this object with intense devotion and we tried many times and in many ways to get a single buffalo to charge our truck while Denys operated the camera. We had most success in the Lake Narton area at the lower end of the Rift Valley wall. But we were never able to overcome the difficulty of the cloud of dust raised by the herd—indeed in one instance the herd was so blinded by the cloud of dust it created that a young bull ran straight on to our truck. It straddled the bonnet. I heard the crumpling of metal and jumped from my seat at the wheel to kill it with an immediate frontal shot before we found ourselves crushed beneath its weight.

After that we tried other tactics. There are clumps of reeds on the north side of the lake offering ample cover for sneaking up on herds of buffalo. In addition, Denys and I camouflaged ourselves with the long grasses.

We spotted a bull with a fine pair of horns—he looked

a real fighter—and headed him off from the main herd, knowing that as soon as he found himself pursued by the truck he would head for heavy cover. I drove the truck and pursued the bull across open country at a steady twenty miles an hour, not wanting to tax his strength. Then he turned off and headed for a solitary tree, beneath which he stood facing us defiantly. Denys got his camera into action and I drove round and round the bull, hoping to goad him into a charge; but although he made one or two feints towards us he would not press them home and in the end we had to give him best and drive off—with some good pictures but not the pictures of the charging beast that Denys really wanted. I wish that we had tried harder on that occasion, for no other opportunity came his way.

A few days later a Masai herdsman carrying a long-bladed spear arrived at our camp in a great state of agitation. Two lions had been attacking and killing his cows and all his efforts to drive them off had been to no avail. Would we help?

Denys and I jumped at the chance. Hurriedly we prepared and made our way across the Uaso Nyiro stream. When we reached the herdsman's land we saw the cattle stampeding in their alarm. The sounds of their terror could be heard a long way off. Clouds of dust choked us as the cows raced round and round in panic, their tails slashing and their hooves making the ground tremble. Their nostrils flared as the smell of lions came to them on the wind and they bucked in fear from the bloodied patch of ground where the marauders had made their kill.

Denys and I made for the scrub where the cattle had been grazing when attacked. The Masai sprinted ahead. In his despair he was trying to hurry us on and shout over his shoulder that the lions had killed five head of his cattle in two days. He had seen them with his own eyes jump on the backs of the victims, which, panic-stricken into a mad gallop, had their heads forced round by the attacker, thus causing them to stumble and break their necks as they fell. Then the lions ripped the bodies to pieces and dragged away what they couldn't eat on the spot. It was the usual method. Lions are masters of this cunning art of allowing the victim to kill himself.

Suddenly I heard Denys cry, 'There they are!' and point away over to the right.

The two lions were only a few yards off. Denys loped towards them on his long legs, raising the double-barrelled rifle he carried. From where I was a few yards behind him I saw the two lions rear up on their hind legs as they prepared to dash Denys to the ground. If they had been a bit quicker I could have done nothing to save him, for he was in my line of fire.

But Denys was quicker than the lions. I saw him stop, shoulder his rifle . . . two shots rang out with scarcely a fraction of time between them. Both lions fell to the ground immediately, one of them first performing a miniature death dance as he fell.

'Good effort,' I said.

'I'd take any chance with you behind me, J.A.,' Denys replied.

That was the last time he and I hunted together.

A while later we met again at Voi, where I was preparing to leave on *safari* with Lea Hudson, an American visitor. Lea, Denys and I were entertained at a party given by the District Commissioner and Denys told us that he was flying up to Nairobi in the morning in his Puss Moth to make arrangements for a *safari* of his own.

Lea and I left fairly early, for we wanted to be away without delay in the morning. Denys came and waved us off. The District Commissioner's wife had given him a great armful of oranges and he stood at the door of the bungalow with the light reflected brightly from the fruit.

He was staying the night with the D.C. and we shouted back at him not to be late in the morning.

At 8 a.m. Lea and I were all ready to go. Suddenly he drew my attention to clouds of black smoke rising from the nearby aerodrome. Fearing the worst we hurried to the scene. We were too late: Denys had crashed during his take-off, the plane was a blazing inferno, and as we watched in horror, held off by the intense heat, a few blackened oranges rolled out from the wreckage.

Denys opened up the Masai reserve with me; he was fearless and fair, and it was fitting that his remains should be buried in the land in which we had both found so much delight. He lies there on the edge of the Ngong hills. A stone marks the spot but nothing memorable is written upon it. He was an undaunted hunter whose memory I cherish in my heart.

How true it is that no prodding of the memory is needed to recall the great companionships of the hunting game.

I am thinking now of Colonel Sandy Macnab, a great American whose forebears hailed from the Scottish highlands. He died a short while ago in America, one of the last of the great hunters of the old school, after a long and happy life in the army and in Africa where there was every opportunity for the sport he loved.

Like all great sportsmen Sandy was a lover of firearms of all kinds and never failed to keep his many weapons in spotless condition—'One day, J.A., my life may depend on the cleanliness of a gun.'

As a revolver shot Sandy achieved perfection, largely due to his training in the American army. His preference was always for the Smith and Wesson .357, a heavy charge revolver which I have seen him use with deadly accuracy on guinea fowl and African francolin.

He enjoyed the thrills of tracking down an animal to its lair or cover far more than the modern method of pursuit by jeep or truck. Curiously, motor-cars seldom cause any consternation among wild beasts. They will stand and stare at the metal monster in their midst without the slightest signs of agitation, presumably taking it for some other species of animal and caring little for the smell of petrol fumes which conveniently mask the human odour of the passengers. Sandy saw little justice in such advantageous methods of hunting. His was the pleasure that increases with difficulty, and the pretty problems posed by changing breezes when he was trying to keep down-wind of the animal he was hunting were a source of joy to him.

There was an occasion when I was with him when we came quite suddenly on a fine pair of lions—one of them sporting a wonderful tawny mane such as is the ambition of every hunter to possess (the black-maned variety is even more coveted, but these are seldom seen outside the National Parks).

We sneaked up on the pair without discovery and were within easy range when they spotted us. They quickly made off and Sandy insisted on giving them a fair chance to escape. He never felt much thrill in shooting a stationary animal because very little skill is involved. At about twenty yards he took aim and fired. We watched the tawny-maned lion leap in its stride, swing round and collapse—shot through the heart.

The other lion immediately bolted and we soon lost sight of it. But when we camped that night we could hear its grunts as it searched for its dead companion. Our native bearers went through their usual performance of coughs and splutterings to scare the beast away. But the sounds of its search went on all night long. We knew from experience that it might stay in the area for several days, indifferent to its own hunger in its desire to trace its mate.

At 7 a.m. in the morning we started off in search,

taking our direction from the sound of the last grunts.
Mount Kilimanjaro rose in snow-capped glory and we
went silently in the direction of our quarry. We sat down
on the fallen limb of a tree to listen, saying nothing in
case the sound of our voices should carry. Our native
tracker shinned up a tree and in a few moments des-
cended and signed to us that he had spotted the lion
moving towards a belt of scrub. We pressed on and came
to his pug marks. These grew fainter as the ground
became harder and we were busily engaged in trying to
pick up the spoor when quite suddenly the lion let out
a tremendous roar only a few yards ahead of us and
began to dash away, keeping closely to every scrap of
cover.

We knew now exactly what its plan was. Lions are
expert at ambushing and it behoves the tracker to keep
a wary eye in circumstances where revenge is the motive.

Slowly we went on, now catching a glimpse of movement ahead, now to the side; but all movements were
so well controlled and concealed that the effect was of
the quarry being in two places at once. Such stalking is
very nerve-racking, for there is always the hidden fear
that the lion has somehow doubled back unobserved and
may be behind instead of ahead. One has to have a lot of
confidence in oneself.

Not a whisper of wind ruffled the foliage as we moved
forward, inch by inch. Cover was thicker now, the lion
had led us into terrain where every advantage was his.
I dared not glance at Sandy, nor he at me, for to take
our eyes from the way ahead might prove fatal. One
thing was certain: the lion, wherever he might be concealed, was aware of our every move.

Immediately ahead was a thick mass of vegetation;
only a few yards separated us from these thick square
bushes. I felt that we were being watched from there;
and as if in confirmation there came on the down-wind

a sudden pungent odour—the unmistakable whiff of the lion's breath, clammy and repugnant.

I nudged Sandy and at the same moment glimpsed a tawny flash behind the screen of bushes.

For a moment of time the lion hung poised in mid-air growling savagely, its mighty leap directed at Sandy. The jaws were opened wide, the amber eyes bulged, the claws outspread. A shattering roar sounded from Sandy's rifle and the lion somersaulted once in mid-air and fell dead between us, blood spurting from the gaping wound above the eye. I had not fired, nor even raised my rifle.

Sandy looked down at the crumpled body. 'The king of beasts de-crowned,' he remarked, and we immediately set to on a long technical chat about the merits of differing guns and shots in dealing with charging lions. He agreed with me that for sheer stopping power against lion or leopard it was hard to beat a 12-bore d/b shotgun firing a charge of S.S.G. pellets, fifteen to the ounce and enough power to break a lion's skull at fifteen yards. Also, the 12-bore comes up to the shoulder easily, one loses no time sighting, and the two cartridges can be fired almost simultaneously.

That lion in full charge was Sandy's last. He decided that he'd shot all the beasts he wanted and would now spend the rest of his days shooting game scenes with his ciné camera and indulge in an occasional fowl for the pot—shot on the wing with his twenty-gauge.

He kept his word. But I saw him many times after that; indeed I quite often used to watch him at his early morning shoot. There were water furrows in Masai where sand grouse would appear in unbelievable numbers every morning around 7 a.m. For a few minutes the sky would be black with them and when they alighted it would appear that to find room for one more bird on the banks and the flats beyond would be impossible.

Sandy would bang off his Winchester pump 20-bore and
take from the mass flying overhead the brace of birds he
wanted for himself. Then he would bring out his ciné
camera and go in search of some unusual picture. He
never in his life lusted after killing things for what some
hunters euphemistically call 'practice' sake'.

His eye for the unusual and beautiful was unerring;
and he was always grateful to me for suggesting a
particular region of the Kilimanjaro area curiously
enough still undiscovered by most travellers—Kimana,
on the foot slopes of the great mountain. Here the
Machagga and Masai tribes live peacefully together,
cultivating the rich soil and growing acres of coffee of a
very high quality. The great trees are filled with song-
birds and pigeons; and wild flowers, including some of
the most exotic orchids I have ever seen, cover the slopes.
A clear-flowing stream of icy water serves the area and
flows on down to the flat land of Kimana swamp, where
buffalo and hippo are as numerous as I have ever known
them in a small area.

All this was the breath of life to Sandy. Plain, swamp
and bush made his natural home, and natives were
always his friends—except insofar as his disgust with
their cooking caused him mistakenly to try and belabour
some sense of cleanliness into them. But they continued
to cough and spit while they were preparing food, and I
think it will take a long time to get them out of ways that
by English standards are revolting.

Sandy took with him from Masailand at least one
unique picture in his ciné camera. He was accompanied
on one *safari* by Sydney Downey, another great professional hunter, when they saw a herd of giraffes which
included an albino specimen. Spotless and uncannily
white this curious creature moved wraithlike among its
companions. Sandy was able to get some excellent shots,
and when he wrote to me after leaving Africa he often

asked if I or anyone else had come across the white giraffe again. But to my knowledge no one has seen it since. There is a rumour that a Dutch hunter shot it in Tanganyika, but the area referred to is some nine hundred miles away from Masailand—in my opinion an abnormally long distance for any giraffe to travel. Aside from this rumour, there is the possibility that an albino specimen would in time achieve its natural coloration; but this I think highly improbable. Much more likely of course is that the famous but elusive white giraffe was killed and eaten by a lion. Unless—a pleasantly sinister thought—it was itself the ghostly manifestation of a giraffe that had already been violently killed and returned to haunt the plains.

Sandy left Africa to go and live in Black Point, Honolulu; and from there he returned to his native United States, where he died only a short while ago at the age of eighty-plus. I have as souvenirs his .375 magnum Hoffmann rifle and his 30/06 Winchester, which I value greatly. He was a great man, a great hunter, bluff and hearty and a splendid companion. And it may be said of him with truth that he never in his life retreated by so much as an inch from danger. I shall not forget that picture of him I have in my mind when the avenging lion sprang from cover in its great leap towards him— the snarling fangs bared and the claws outspread. For I have in my time seen a Masai spearman, the bravest of the brave, torn and shaken by an enraged lion and later weeping with the pain brought by poisoning to the lacerations from the claws that have ripped at rotting flesh. And Sandy escaped that injury and pain only by the quickness of hand and eye and the reliability of a superb and superbly kept weapon.

A good many people have asked me about fear—don't I ever feel it? It's one of those conversational gambits which don't mean very much, being designed, with small talk, to keep social life going, and it doesn't need a very closely considered answer. In any case this isn't the place for dissertations on human emotions, nor am I the man to give them. But I can give a short answer and an exemplary incident.

The answer—Yes; the incident belonging to my early days, when I was no longer a greenhorn but had not yet learnt shrewd judgement.

At that time East Africa was wrung by a great drought. Water-holes had dried up and the courses that drained the land were crumbling and riven with widening cracks. Men were sorely tried, but beasts were desperate and had taken on an unaccustomed savagery.

My camp was a lonely one, a single tent pitched a short distance away from Mackinnon Road railway station. There was a water tank sunk in level with the surface, and this served the station and the needs of the few people nearby. The tank had a corrugated iron lid which was kept bolted down.

The weather was changing and rain was clearly on the way; but for many days now it had held off, leaving the atmosphere damp and misty—exactly the kind of African weather which incites beasts to unease and fear.

The brief twilight gave way to complete darkness and I sat in my tent listening to the distant sound of lions, modulating uneasily between whining and anger. I could not be sure whether they were coming nearer or going farther away; but I did know that animals tortured by thirst will detect the smell of water from several miles.

When I went outside my tent I knew that rain would come very soon now. There was a drizzle in the air. I was quite alone; and in a moment I heard the snarling of lions quite near—or could it be that they were farther away than I thought and that the sound was carried more easily on the heavy air? I could not be sure. But I made myself stand there and listen for a prolonged moment. And suddenly out of the darkness a sound came and I was quite certain: there were lions nearby—perhaps they were padding towards the water tank this very minute. I peered through the darkness, imagining that perhaps I should see their eyes gleaming; but there was nothing but the impenetrable dark and the almost indistinguishable shape of the tent behind me as I turned, feeling a prickling down my back.

Inside the tent there was no comfort now—I was better outside, for at least I wouldn't have the tent collapse on top of me, which might, I imagined, happen if one of the lions took it into his head to attack in desperation. Besides, the stillness was unbearable. I wanted to go out and bang on the corrugated lid of the tank, shout, do anything that would end this unnatural silence.

But in a moment there was no need for that. Chaos, the frenzied roaring of lions, sounded at my very door. The sound was terrifying. Africa seemed at that moment a very small place, walled-in by thirst-maddened beasts.

I forced myself to look out. I could see no clear shapes, but it seemed to me that there were three lions there at the tank, their outburst of fury due to their frustration at being unable to get at the water they knew very well was there.

Nowadays I know that lions do not trouble a hoot about a lone human being at night. They seem to know that shooting is impossible, and unless hungry because unable to catch something more palatable (as in the case of the lion tortured by embedded porcupine quills) they take very little interest in mankind. But on that occasion I couldn't be sure of this. Somehow or other I believed it inherently, but I dared not trust my intuition. I did realize, though, that it was quite impossible, as well as foolish, for me to stand there and do nothing.

Trusting to luck and judgement I ran across the few yards between me and the tank. Would I be able to find and draw the bolt? What if one or all the lions were standing on the lid? What if one of them—but by this time I had come to the tank. I was lucky: the lions had prowled a few feet off. I could hear their claws tapping on the concrete surround of the tank; and a whiff of sour breath came at me as one of the beasts turned its head in surprise as I knelt and fiddled with the bolt—which, praise be, I had found at the first attempt. I remember thinking that smell was exactly like that of the sickly gum that oozes from acacia trees.

I drew the bolt and flung the lid back with a flourish. It made a great clatter as it fell, and at this the lions suddenly began roaring again—angrily and only a foot or two from me.

I turned and bolted back to my tent. In a minute the roaring and snarling died away and was replaced by the sound of lapping as the beasts took their fill.

As soon as they were satisfied they went on their way without further ado. But it was well I hadn't thwarted them. I can remember only too clearly, to this day, the fear that the reverberations of their roaring inspired in me. The sound is, I think, even more terrible than the trumpeting of elephants.

I must speak in this chapter of another great man of the hunting game, this time a native of the Wakamba tribe, Detei, who went on many *safaris* with me as a scout.

Detei was a loyal and courageous man who for eight years had managed to avoid death and even serious injury by hairbreadth escapes but whom I never found wanting in enthusiasm for a new hunt. Elephant and rhino were his speciality, and like most of his tribe he had inherited the hunting instinct and was adept at stalking his quarry so stealthily that he could get close enough for a single well-placed shot to bring off the kill.

I trained him in the use of modern rifles and he always

had a preference for the single barrel weapon with magazine action. He never forgot the golden rule I made him repeat again and again—that in attack one must keep one's eyes unswervingly on the target and concentrate all thought on placing the shot so that a kill is made first time. One must be compassionate and at the same time avoid the dangerous consequences of merely wounding a beast.

Detei was a simple, God-fearing soul and I found his charm endearing. He was typical of his tribe in his simplicity and loyalty and would always go out of his way to help me in any difficulties I encountered.

When he heard that three rhinos had become a source of danger to the people of a tiny village ten miles or so from Makindu he came and told me and asked if we could go in pursuit. It seemed that the rhinos had lately been attacking the village women who were going peacefully about their domestic chores—particularly when they were drawing water and carrying it home in gourds. Returning from the streams carrying their gourds they would be quite unable to move quickly and the rhinos would emerge from nearby cover and gore them in their well-proportioned buttocks. This naturally incurred the wrath of women and husbands who now requested protection—and death to the sour-tempered beasts.

Detei and a fellow native scout started off at crack of dawn. Luck came to them early and Detei encountered one of the wanted trio—a mature bull—in a tangled thicket on the outskirts of the village. It was busily chewing sapless thorn when the scouts came upon it and looked up in surprise as Detei levelled his rifle. A second later it dropped dead.

At the sound of the shot a number of tick birds, which had been busily engaged on picking the parasites from the backs of several other rhinos a little distance off, rose in flight. The flurry of birds gave the alarm to a cow and calf rhino which immediately galloped off, heading for the refuge of denser thicket across the plain.

Unperturbed Detei and his fellow scout followed. It was some distance and the ground was hard and dry, but eventually they picked up the spoor and entered the thicket.

The density of the thorn precluded any possibility of good vision and they were forced to stand and peer about them for the quarry. Unhappily the wind had changed and the rhinos had become aware of their pursuers' presence. Immediately the cow rhino charged from a very short distance ahead, and such is their mobility in even the densest scrub that they were upon the two scouts before there was the slightest possibility of taking aim or even raising the rifles.

The second scout was able to jump aside; but Detei was not so fortunate: he was hemmed in by the thorn and could not move quickly enough in any direction. The thundering beast came down upon him, its great foot giving him a powerful blow at the side of the neck, breaking it instantly.

When we found him he was on his knees with his rifle still in his hands. But its barrel was choked with earth; he had not had time to raise it but had fallen forward upon it as the rhino's hoof came down on him.

Detei's was a hunter's destiny and a hunter's death. Brief and unspectacular, unknown and unmarked save by a handful of people who saw him buried in Makindu cemetery, it was nonetheless a death belonging in the annals of hunting history, and I am glad I have recorded it and in my very small way paid homage to him. He was a great hunter.

MANHUNT VI

THE CHASE CONTINUED

At Makindu I found great excitement. The aerodrome, which is normally used only as an emergency landing strip and a take-off point for private charter companies, had been the scene of a noteworthy event. A private plane had touched down and gone again almost immediately. I didn't need to ask who the passenger was. Rammal had tricked me nicely. By now he was on his way to Mombasa where he would doubtless reorganize his plans for the shipment of Benares ware.

Furious with myself for being so easily taken in and disappointed that I'd not after all had to cope with another Darajani man-eater, I went over to the radio operator's cabin.

'I suppose that ruddy Indian's in Mombasa by now?'

He shook his head and pointed to the spare chair that was tucked in amongst a muddle of batteries, boxes of spare parts and tools.

'No. Sit down for a bit. The pilot's having trouble of some kind—carburettor jet, he thinks. He's returning here, not quite sure if he can make it. I'm in touch . . .'

This put a very different complexion on things and I felt myself cheering up. Learning that Rammal had eluded me had aroused a new kind of excitement in me. I had to admit I'd been indifferent—or at any rate not positively interested—before; but the indignation aroused by an easy defeat is fairly strong. I was feeling at that moment strongly anti-Rammal. And it seemed as if I might have another chance—though I didn't deserve it.

The operator fiddled with the apparatus. I could hear

nothing but a faint humming from the power unit. Then he started calling the plane.

'Makindu to Charter Abel, Makindu to Charter Abel. What is your position now? Over.'

Communication was established. It seemed that the plane was still in difficulties, heading for home with a misfiring engine.

'He's over the Chyulu Range, west of here, trying to glide in but not having much luck because of the air currents. He's losing height too. I'd better alert an ambulance. Looks as if he might crash on the hill slopes.'

'I'll get out there,' I said. 'Will you warn the D.C.'s office that Rammal's aboard?'

I drove the International westward out of Makindu across the plain towards Chyulu. The foothills of the forty-mile range gleamed whitely in the afternoon sunlight. The mountains rose from a rocky plateau which was a favourite resort of lions, and as I bumped on over the poorly defined track I saw one magnificent beast lying calmly viewing me from a short distance off. He might have been the prototype of Landseer's lions in Trafalgar Square—supine, majestic, and quite uninterested in the passage of the truck. Farther off two others roamed towards me across the plain.

But I had no time to bother with lions now. I could hear the plane very faintly when I reduced the roar of my own engine, and when I took a look from the cab I saw it hovering over Chyulu—very tiny as yet but even at that distance betraying its engine difficulties.

Looking round, I could see that the pilot was going to have a lot of difficulty touching down here if he couldn't make Makindu. The airstrip was only a couple of miles behind me, but judging from the uneven flight the craft was making the deciding issue would be a matter of yards rather than miles. All round there was nothing but ledges and ridges of rock and scrubland. Although in general terms one might refer to the approach to Chyulu as flat land it was not by any means flat from the point of view of an aircraft's pilot. The few level patches were divided by bits of escarpment and cliff which increased the hazards of limping down on to what would appear from the air a bit of ground no bigger than a postage stamp. The pilot's best bet obviously was to make for one of the more extensive stretches which were far from even—and indeed were strewn with boulders—but which might at least offer a bit of space for manœuvring.

The machine was almost overhead now. I could hear its engine choking and see it riding bumpily from right to left across my own direction of movement. When I looked I saw it was heading for a stretch of plateau where there was at least a run in with the wind in the favourable direction if he could bank and turn and come in towards me from the left. It was chancy—an ugly escarpment of scrub-covered rock divided the available space however he approached it. The only question was, would he attempt his landing on the side of the escarpment nearest to me? If so, he'd have a rather better chance, I judged; because from the escarpment to the track I was travelling along and for a good couple of hundred yards on the other side of the track there wasn't anything very serious to impede his progress. But if he landed on the far side of the escarpment he might very easily crash into it.

I turned off the track and bumped over the rocky and drought-hardened ground. I was now travelling towards the escarpment. The plane was going the same way, very low, it couldn't have been more than thirty feet, with its engine silent now except for occasional spasmodic coughs and whirrings of the airscrew. If the pilot couldn't get it to rise he'd hit the escarpment, surely.

It was at that moment I saw the lioness.

She was poised on the escarpment at its point of chamfering-off to ground level, on a flattened eminence, and she was not alone: her twin cubs, I could see now, were milling around her playfully. A little higher up the escarpment her mate, a not very impressively maned lion, prowled to and fro in obvious annoyance at the sight and sound of the plane. This was something they couldn't be indifferent to. A road vehicle—yes; but this was far too threatening and too close. I heard the lioness grunt angrily, and her mate answered with a louder but not very convincing roar.

Then the pilot managed a smart bit of manœuvring: the nose of the plane tilted upward at the very last minute and it was across the escarpment. Both lions now gave full-throated growls, and this started the other wanderers grunting and growling. It sounded as I pushed on across the rocks, tilting this way and that in the groaning International, as if there were lions on every quarter; but when I took a quick look out of the cabin window I could see only three besides the family standing angrily on the escarpment; but they were coming in quite close in a threatening way. They certainly wouldn't attack the truck, but I had to think of the possibility of the plane crashing. However, that was something to consider when the time came. At the moment I was bothering about the plane staying up at all.

But as I watched I saw it rise again a little, quite sharply, bank and turn. It was trying to turn favourably to the wind. And it was round!—coming straight towards me apparently dead certain at the moment to crash into the escarpment just about where the lioness stood grunting angrily.

But no. Once again the pilot's skill served him well. The engine coughed into one of its momentary spasms of life and the craft rose a few feet, bumping unstably.

For a second or two I held my breath. From where I sat in the truck it looked exactly as if the plane was going to run full tilt into the lioness and her cubs.

But it didn't, quite. There was this momentary hesitation as the machine tilted. It was perhaps eight feet above the pride of lions on their eminence and it seemed to hang there helplessly.

Then the lioness acted. I could see her anger venting itself in the snarling jaws and flicking tail. Her cubs—which weren't so very small—pressed closely against her sides. But passive resistance against the roaring monster that hung suspended above her didn't suit her at all. She rose to her hind legs and I saw her scrape furiously at the unsteadily suspended machine. Her judgement and her anger were precisely timed: her scimitar claws caught and ripped at the port-side wing. I saw the stiffened canvas tear away, the whole plane heel over so that the wing-tip touched a boulder.

It was all over in a second. Before the lioness, waving the ripped-away canvas like a flag, had regained her all-fours position the plane had pancaked to the ground twenty yards ahead of me. I heard the undercarriage split and crack and a long tearing clash as the plane hit the ground.

Immediately a great cloud of dust obscured my view. A fusillade of small stones rattled on the truck. I braked hard and waited for the explosion and the livid flowering of flame. But none came. The clashing sound of the impact died away and the dust sank slowly, silting into the cab and thinning like mist as it settled. The grittiness of it was pricking at my eyes.

I got down and went towards the plane, still expecting the explosion. But none came. There was a complete silence except for the thin twanging of one of the broken control wires on the plane. The lions that had been closing in were now loping away across the plain. As the dust settled the aircraft emerged as if from a cloud of steam. It had slewed round and come to rest at right angles to its line of flight, tilting sideways on to one smashed wing. The other wing rose grotesquely into the air with its underside canvas flapping in rags where it had been ripped by the lioness.

Miraculously, the engine still hadn't caught fire; and as I reached the plane I saw the pilot, his face grey with dust, climb out of the wreckage.

AN ADVENTURE WITH CROCODILES

GENERALLY speaking dangers appear much greater in retrospect. Crises recollected in tranquillity inspire one to marvel at one's ability to cope with fantastic circumstances and insuperable difficulties. The truth is, of course, that one is prepared up to a point which is relative to one's experience and character. After that— destiny, the luck of the moment . . . and, of course, the fact that in the midst of danger one seldom has the time or the inclination to philosophize or compare.

That pilot whom I now ran forward to assist, for example, had just been through what should have been one of the most terrifying experiences given to man. To hover uncertainly between heaven and earth and to be ninety-nine per cent certain of death implies a state of mind given over to stark terror; yet in the event he would have been far more concerned with the mechanics of manœuvring his plane to think consciously of his situation as any kind of moral crisis. The automatic reactions of his skill, perhaps the desperate summoning of reserves of physical strength, and the luck of the gods. Sober apprehension of mutilation or death would not come till afterwards.

Later, when I checked with him about his feelings and

referred in what I hope was an understandingly flippant way to the bravery that would undoubtedly be attributed to him I found that his analysis of men's reactions to danger was nearly enough the same as mine. In fact he merely threw the ball back to my end of the ground by asking, 'What about the tight spots you've been in yourself? Did you think of them in a detached way?'

And of course he was right: I never had. Anyway not till afterwards.

There was, for example, one situation I found myself in which seems either incredible or plain miraculous whenever I think about it, but which at the time inspired very few emotions—certainly not including excitement— even though in retrospect it looks pretty hair-raising.

An Italian Count and his Contessa had hired me to conduct them on what they termed a 'crocodile outing'. A hunt, they said, was altogether too violent a word to apply to what they had in mind. 'We wish to catch one, perhaps two, crocodilla and study the ways of these interesting creatures the crocodilla.'

The best place for crocodiles within reasonable distance at that time was a stretch of the Semliki river on the borders of Uganda and the Belgian Congo. The point I had in mind is at the southern end of Lake Albert, where the delta is of sifted mud and sand plus patches of reed and rotting wood and other flotsam washed down from the higher reaches of the river. The reeds and siltings provide a favoured hideout for hundreds of crocodiles, for these creatures love the slime and shaded banks of unfrequented rivers. They are vicious and tough and are able to go for long periods without food. Sooner or later they know a 'ray cow or waterbuck will find its way to the river. These innocent animals never seem to learn the lesson of the crocodile, whose method is to lie submerged only a few inches from the spot where its prey will drink, wait till the buck or cow is actually drinking, and then snap the rack-toothed and immensely powerful jaws on the victim's muzzle. The next step is to drag the helpless beast by the nose down into the water and hold it under till it drowns. This task completed, the crocodile lumberingly emerges from the water on its short legs, dragging the victim which it now stores on the bank in some suitable sunlit hollow where decomposition of the carcass will be very quick. Crocodiles don't eat fresh food; they are able to judge to a nicety the exact degree of gaseous decomposition that pleases their palate; and at that stage they will eat the putrefying flesh. Unpleasant creatures in habit and mien, the scavengers of African inland waters, but valuable commercially for the sake of their neck and belly skins; and offering hunting experiences that might well stand me in good stead on later occasions. So off we went, the Count and his lady, plus a few bearers.

The mud flats were inaccessible to large craft, but for the beginning of our journey we managed to charter a steam tug that would take us down river as far as the delta. From there we would have to hire canoes—craft for which I have an intense dislike—from the Congo fishermen and make our way through the sludge as best we could.

But our enterprise seemed beset by trouble from the very beginning.

Lake Albert is famous for the sudden intense storms that blow across it; and one of these caught us fairly and squarely amidships as we sat in our decrepit tug a few miles up the Semliki. The blackness of the night was riven with a continuous display of the most violent lightning I have ever seen. It was as if the whole great universe of darkness was marbled with vivid red and green and yellow. Tree after tree split and fell and the roars and trumpetings of animals seemed to imply that all the devils of hell were at our very gates.

But this was only the beginning. So far there had been no thunder. Nor rain. Nor wind. They came one by one, each adding its impact to the intensity of a storm we would have said was apocalyptic in its magnitude—if we hadn't been too busy trying to stand, sit or lie with reasonable security in our tug of a steamer.

The wind lashed into a vortex at the heart of Lake Albert and the convulsed water spread northward into the mouth of the Nile and southward into the mouth of the Semliki. Constrained by the river banks, the turbulent waters heaved and rose, lashed by the torrential rain that fell from a sky split and split again by chasms of lightning. The animals were inaudible now. I could imagine the lions in rocky caverns, the elephants herded silently together, their trumpetings silenced by the cymbal clashes of thunder and the whipping of the wind, the birds and monkeys chattering in terror in the swaying treetops.

I say I could have imagined them. It was afterwards I did my imagining, of course. At the time my only concern—and indeed the concern of all of us—was simply to keep out of harm's way.

The tug heaved and rolled so much that there was an ever-present danger of capsizing. Many times during the storm the ship's flat bottom tipped right out of the water. Below, the Count and Contessa and myself fell and were tipped in every possible direction. There was nothing stable to hold on to. Rails and doorknobs that afforded security one minute were wrenched away the next and we found ourselves flung away by a tipping of the ship on to its other side.

I had the utmost admiration for the Contessa. She was a biggish woman, but not by any means built for such buffetings. All the same, she withstood the countless bruisings she received during the night with considerable equanimity considering her Latin temperament; and once, in a moment when the ship was very temporarily upright she peered through the port and exclaimed:

'Hunter—look! Is it not crocodilla?'

She was right. The tug was surrounded by a jammed mass of them. In the blinding streak of lightning that illumined the scene I could see their scaly bodies huddled together like jammed treetrunks, apparently riding the storm with the greatest of enjoyment.

The Count took less kindly to the storm than his wife did. He was sullen and resentful and kept rolling about with his hands on his enormous belly muttering what I took to be Italian imprecations. I didn't take too kindly to it myself. And although the Contessa managed to keep upright longer than any of us even she, as the hours mounted and the storm went thundering on, took on the haunted look of despair.

At dawn the storm ceased quite suddenly. The stability of the ship seemed remarkable. We all went gingerly up to the iron deck and looked around. We discovered each other clinging to the rails and made weak jokes about the storm having a hangover effect on our *status quo*.

The river was now quite tranquil. Only the swirls of mud and scattered débris on the flats and the several charred and stricken trees gave any indication of the storm's severity. The crocodiles had dispersed: they lay all round, sunning themselves on the steaming delta, their tails thumping the sand and their jaws wickedly snapping as they watched us with their malevolent little eyes.

The Count and Contessa went below to rest awhile. A multitude of duck came winging up from the south; they were like a vibrant cloud and the sound of their cries and the beat of their wings reminded me that a brace or two would be welcome for the dinner table. As I bagged them the shots roused the crocodiles to sudden activity. Hundreds of them began to swarm down to the river on their grotesque legs and within a few minutes the mass

of them began to seethe downstream. They swam submerged, very fast, the protruding knobs above their eyes
perforating the surface like thousands of hailstones.
Clearly, we had come to the right place.

After our meal we went ashore and made arrangements with the native fishermen for the hire of a canoe.
These hollowed-out treetrunks seem to me to be the
last word in discomfort. They're uncomfortable to sit in
because of the restricted space, difficult to navigate, and
easy to capsize. But there was no other form of transport
that would get us up the delta, so we had to settle for
the biggest one we could find. Even this wasn't big enough
in the beam to accommodate the Count, who regretfully
decided that the Contessa and I should make the journey
while he remained at headquarters on the tug.

We took two native guides to do the poling for us and
set off. I could not help but admire the game way the
Contessa agreed to try everything once. She, being a big
woman—though admittedly not on the same scale as her
husband—fitted very ill into the narrow canoe; for that
matter, I'm not all that small myself and couldn't claim
to be at all comfortable; but she caught the humour of
the situation, and between wriggles to ease her sorely
pressed buttocks she grimaced at me—wriggling with
equal discomfort at the other end of the canoe—and
laughed quite heartily at the misery she had brought on
herself by her determination to indulge in a 'crocodilla
outing'.

We had good going for three hours or so. The natives
never relaxed in their efforts. Their poling was effective
not only in propelling us down river towards Lake
Albert, but also in giving the canoe a continuous disconcerting wobble which they seemed to delight in. The
Contessa and I exchanged more grimaces: neither of us
felt happy wobbling from side to side in this unseemly
fashion. But there was nothing to be done.

We were by now approaching Lake Albert. Here the river widened, but there was still very little depth to it. Islands and banks of reed and tall grasses stretched away on either side of us. Herds of hippos watched our progress with comic gloom, their great jowls gleaming with mud, tick birds arrayed in hundreds on their broad backs. At one spot a group of young elephants drank and splashed noisily on the banks.

As we rounded a bend of the river I saw the Contessa give me an anxious look and point ahead.

The river just ahead of us was jammed tight with crocodiles. They play partially submerged, their great jaws snapping and their tails lashing the water. And as we went on, propelled by the strong current—the natives had seen the danger and stopped poling—we were suddenly in the midst of them. One would have said it was impossible to work the smallest log into the space between the crocs, but there we were in our treetrunk canoe looking all round us at this packed mass of flailing yellowish green tails, the rack teeth and the wickedly flickering eyelids of hundreds of reptiles which, though not normally man-eating, would certainly not be over particular about feeding off a bit of human flesh.

I knew that the immediate danger would arise as much from their fear as from their malevolence. Normally crocodiles, like most wild beasts, scatter in alarm at the sight of human beings. We'd seen an example of that earlier in the morning when they'd heard the sound of my gunshots. But wedged as tightly as they were I realized that any massed retreat on their part could result only in our being capsized by the flailing tails.

And so it proved. I yelled to the natives to ram their poles into the river bed and cling on, hoping that we'd at least achieve some kind of security. But it was too late: alarm had become translated into movement. There was a tumultuous heaving of the bodies all round us. Tails lashed wildly in the air and one great croc snapped menacingly at our canoe. I need hardly say that he could have pulled it, and us, below the surface without the slightest effort. As it was, he missed. But our narrow, keelless craft was already beginning to heave and roll; and suddenly the inevitable happened: we were caught by a single great swipe of scaly tail.

For a second or two we rocked and I thought we'd survived; but the crocodiles were now swarming in movement against the sides of the canoe and the weight of those nearest to us was quite enough to capsize us completely.

This meant in effect not that we sank at once into the water but that we were all pitched out on to the moving crocs, their backs and tails and top jaws forming an unstable landing place.

It was a disconcerting experience. For myself, I was not so badly off. The crocodile I happened to land on immediately submerged in fright, leaving me floundering in the thick scummy water; but the Contessa and the natives were not so lucky. The Contessa, so far as I could see, was lying almost horizontally across the jaws of another croc a few yards away. She too was floundering about, and I could see that in a very short time she'd be lashed by one of the flailing monsters or crunched between racks of teeth.

I trod bottom and tried to reach her; but I literally had to push at the crocs all round me. And I seemed to be so caught up in their midst that I was being forced away from her.

At that moment she rolled off and was herself submerged. With an effort I managed to reach out and grab her arm and drag her towards me. The natives now had got themselves into a less populated part of the river and were striking out towards the bank. I managed to get a

little nearer the Contessa and we stood upright in the
river as the great exodus of crocodiles went on past us.

There was nothing at all we could do. At any minute
the current might force us down into the water, a pair
of jaws snap at our limbs or a tail lash us to death. But
we stood clinging there minute after minute while the
great sea of reptiles swam past us on their way to less
disturbed shores. And the luck of the gods was with us.
Our time had not come. For after what seemed endless
suspense we realized that there were few crocodiles
around us, that the majority had already lashed their
way down river, and that we were within treading distance of a reed-covered island against which the canoe—
upside down but undamaged—had miraculously come
to rest.

And all that time I was not nearly so conscious of the
danger we were in as of my own inadequacy. It is only
now that I look back that I truly comprehend the real
danger that beset us. A tight spot indeed. But to be in a
tight spot without any means of defence at all, to be at
the mercy of forces and creatures outside one's control—
this is the sort of tight spot that makes me sweat a bit
when I consider it in retrospect. At the time, though, I'm
sure it was my defencelessness, and to a certain extent
my undignified stance, in the middle of a muddy river
with a clinging Contessa, as the crocodiles buffeted past
us, that seemed to me most important—and far more real
than the threat of death.

When we were at last back on the tug the Contessa
seemed none the worse and none the less keen. I'd supposed she'd have had enough of crocodiles for one day;
but not her!

'These crocodilla, Hunter—they were the biggest you
ever saw?'

'Not the biggest. But big enough in the circumstances.'

'But the biggest—where were they?'

So I had to tell her about earlier days when I was a learner. One is always a learner at the hunting game, but in this case I knew nothing at all of crocodiles; and with the brash enthusiasm of the ignorant I set out to capture a monster.

I'd heard about the ton-weight creatures of Lake Victoria, Uganda, and I had reliable information that Kabanga Bay, on the north side of the great lake, was as good a spot as any I'd find if I was after a record skin. I was. I wanted them for a museum, and only outstanding specimens would qualify in this case.

Hilda, my wife, came with me on this *safari*, and at the first camp we pitched we were cursed night and day by mosquitoes. It was impossible to stay there and next day we moved farther inland. It was too far really, but there was no alternative, and I had to spend most of that day getting back with my bearers and equipment to the bay.

I had my plan all ready: I would shoot a hippo, drag it on to the bank and simply wait for the crocs to come and gorge. It all sounded so easy. I had visions of my name in Rowland Ward's book of game records, I was certainly determined that the biggest croc ever was already mine.

I shot the hippo all right—with some regret, for these clumsy water horses are benign by nature and their short tusks, which are not of ivory but of bone, have little commercial value: besides, there's something simple-minded about them, though they can be agile enough in their responses if they're really frightened or roused in anger. But they're convenient as bait, and the old fellow I shot was more or less near the end of his days by my judgement. He was yawning widely and I shot him before he got his great mouth shut again.

I'd also been bright enough to arrange a lighter with an outboard motor to tow the hippo to the place where

I'd set up my camp. That way the crocs would come to me and I wouldn't have to put up with the dreadful plague of mosquitoes.

I looped the tow rope round the carcass and off we went—the carcass now buoyant with the accumulating gases inside it and floating like a cork. I kept looking to and fro across the bay, expecting to see crocs by the score following in my wake. But not one. I knew nothing at that time about their preference for rotting corpse meat.

On the north side of the bay I found a tree with a convenient lookout nook about ten feet up and made fast the carcass to the trunk with twenty yards of the two-inch tow-rope. The hippo, now blown up like an enormous balloon, was smelling strongly by this time. Very unpleasant. And as the hours went by it became worse. Not only that, the wind bore all the stink up to my hideout and made me feel very sickly. Also, there were the mosquitoes: they, or some like them, seemed to have followed me around. I felt very depressed; and several times during the night—neither small nor large crocodiles having been within miles of me—I wondered whether I'd pack up and go home. Then there'd be a change in the wind and the stupefying stench would get wafted away from me and I'd remember that there was really quite a lot at stake and that if I couldn't stand the smell of corpse rot better than that I'd never make much of a hunter. Anyway, I stayed on all next day and night, watching the carcass distend to bursting point and the late stages of internal decomposition set in. This was marked by the thousands of bluebottles that swarmed round the anus, nostrils, eyes and ears and feasted on the maggoty rot that had spread outwards from those parts.

By this time the stench—and the mosquitoes—had become so familiar that I could bear them more easily

and I was prepared to wait till something happened—
a week if need be.

But by noon next day I was rewarded. Peering from
my hideout across the lake I saw an armada of crocodiles
approaching, converging upon the carcass like black
sticks that grew bigger and became logs and then live
and threatening; their green, yellow and brown scales
rippling like scraps of coloured glass on the surface of
the lake.

I could feel my heart beating with joy. These were real
monsters—even my unpractised eye could tell that.
Crocodiles keep on growing till they die; these appeared
to be very old indeed.

They were all round the carcass now, clawing and
crawling over it. The flies rose in angrily buzzing clouds:
and to this buzzing and the hoarse grunts of the crocs
was added the hiss of pungent gas escaping from the
punctured flesh. The stench was all but overpowering
and if it hadn't been for my anxiety to make my kills I'd
have passed out with nausea. But I kept my mind on the
job and took careful aim with my Holland and Holland
.375 magnum.

I took my time. There were four particularly fine
specimens which had crawled right on top of the carcass.
One of these was of truly enormous size and kept trying
to push the others out of the way. I could hear the snapping and clicking of teeth as they lunged at each other
and at the same time ripped at the inch-thick flesh as if
it were paper. Very carefully I picked these four off and
shot them through the neck. They all died instantly, their
jaws twitching open and their claws suddenly relaxing
from the shredded flesh. This was all right so far as three
of them were concerned: they simply lay dead on the
deflated hippo carcass. But the fourth, the largest of
them all—my judgement was bad there. I should have
waited till he'd clambered up on the carcass and nosed

his opponents out of the way. I shot him just before he'd got proper purchase, and he began to slip back into the water. Panicking, I fired again, having some sort of notion at the back of my mind of anchoring him. But, of course, it was impossible. The muscular twitchings of death had released his hold and there was no stopping him now. He slid deeper and deeper into the water and in a few minutes there were only a few air bubbles to mark the spot where he'd sunk.

I could have kicked myself for my impatience, but it was no use sulking. I had three good specimens and my immediate job was to get them back to my base camp. I called up my bearers and got them to bring the lighter down. By that time the hippo meat had been divided up into joints by the scrambling crocs and taken away down river to be stored until even more stinking. The dead crocs had been dragged off with ropes by my native boys; and the skeleton of the hippo lay there with vultures scrapping for the few remaining shreds of flesh, their obscene heads bobbing about inside the skeleton like workmen on some vast building project. I scared them off my prize kills only by continually firing at them.

When we got back to base we had a really good examination of the crocs and skinned them. They were fine, aged monsters and I was well pleased; but I regretted the one that got away, for I have never seen a finer or larger.

All in all, as I told the Contessa, Lake Victoria was in many ways finer crocodile country than Semliki. Even after her ordeal she was game enough to say that next time we'd go south.

The Count and Contessa were so fascinated by crocodiles that I had to ply them with stories all the time. Even during the following days of that *safari*, when we went out again and captured several goodish specimens, she still wanted to hear of other crocodile adventures while we sat at our evening meal.

'Hunter, you say these reptilia, these sweet little crocodilla, they last a long time on no food at all. How long? You know?'

As it happened, I didn't know the book answer to that one (I seldom do), but I'd been able to make my own judgement some time before when I'd been accompanying Allan McMartin, a great Canadian sportsman who had taken me on an elephant hunt with him.

We were in the Uaso Nyiro river area of Kenya at the time and had come on a grove of palm trees where we sat down to rest. Nearby there were some huge wild fig trees with the complicated trellis of their roots exposed by the erosion of the river bank; and beneath these roots a subterranean passage into and out of which there was an incessant cloud of blow-flies. We wondered if the carcass of some warthog or python was concealed there and went to investigate. With a long pole we began poking about in the burrow. And presently a large crocodile came crawling out.

He was a pitiful sight: his belly sagged and his eyes were sunken into his shrivelled head, his great tail was flaccid and ravaged by some parasitic disease, and his legs could not support him, so that he was forced to propel himself forward with convulsive jerkings of his hide. The bared teeth, from which the jaw skin had shrunken away, were carious and insect-ridden. We shot the poor creature immediately and then looked round to see if there were any more sufferers. It didn't take us long to find them; there were nine in a very small area along the river bank, all of them having crawled away to die. McMartin reckoned their starvation was due to the prolonged drought which had lowered the level of the river to such an extent that animals had sought water elsewhere and the crocodiles had been deprived of their natural prey.When we worked out the length of the drought period we came to the conclusion that the crocodiles had been at least two months without food. My own view is that they could easily survive one month without harmful effects; and this, compared with most other animals, is a very long time.

It seemed to comfort the Contessa and increase her affection for crocodiles when I told her that they weren't considered revolting creatures by everyone. Not by any means. In the Lake Rukwa area of Tanganyika, for example, I have many times watched perfectly idyllic scenes where native fishermen with their nets spread out all round them made pets of the crocodiles, which swam and plunged about in kittenish ecstasy. And natives of the Sese Islands in Lake Victoria consider the crocodile as a sacred creature. On one island—where there are only twelve native inhabitants—I have actually seen crocodiles called by name and come ashore to flap about beside the natives. A curious hereditary song-call is used in such cases, and I understood that this call had been handed down from father to son for many generations—ever since the days when crocodiles were summoned from the water to attack and tear to pieces those whom the tribe wanted punished.

It is a strange, eerie song—quite tuneless by western standards—but not without a certain hypnotic fascination. Although I tend to be mildly derisive about what novelists refer to as Mysteries of Darkest Africa, I have to admit that there are things which are outside the comprehension of a practical hunter.

MANHUNT VII

THE CAPTURE

I HELPED the pilot over to the International. He was young and as steely-nerved as they come. He didn't really need much of my help. But he was still dubious about the engine.

'It might go up in a sheet of horrible flame at any minute. I can't think why it hasn't already: sheer luck.'

'Skill.'

He shrugged and fumbled in his flying kit till he found a hare's foot which he kissed with all the ardour of a lad kissing his first girl at his first dance.

'Skill, hell. That's my totem. I'm just the same as these African wallahs—we all are in a way. Got to have something to believe in, a bit of a symbol you can carry in your pocket.' He was sitting on the running board of the truck and he glanced up suddenly with apprehension. 'It can't do much good against those ruddy lions, though.' His alarm was genuine, I could tell that. He could defy gravity and the elements with a hare's foot in his pocket but he couldn't believe that a lion was anything but ravenous for his flesh.

'They'll clear off,' I assured him. I shot a round into the air and the lioness and her family trotted off up the escarpment. 'You see? They're just scared and self-defensive. If you whizz about a few feet above them in aeroplanes naturally they're on the defensive. Who wouldn't be?'

He looked ruefully at the damaged plane with its tattered wing. 'I'll bet you've never seen that happen before—lion on hind legs ripping the guts out of flying

crate. God! Nobody'll ever believe it. Wish to heaven
you'd had a camera.' He flung out his arms in declama-
tory fashion. His nerves were reacting a bit now. 'Ladies
and gents, this was a unique occasion, abso-ruddy-lutely
unique, a lion attacking a flying aircraft, and as the
camera cannot lie I can prove it to you——'

I shook my head. 'It wasn't the first time. I——' Then
suddenly I remembered something and got up and ran
to the plane. Rammal! He must still be in there, of
course. In the confusion of the crash and my concern for
the pilot I'd forgotten him.

He was crouching in the passenger seat, pop-eyed with
fear, not knowing whether he was in the air or on the
ground, whether he dared move or whether he ought to
make a run from the thousands of police he probably
thought were awaiting him. His blandness and self-
control had entirely deserted him. He was just a terrified
little Indian storekeeper waiting for instructions.

I got him out with some difficulty. The fuselage of the
plane had twisted badly as a result of the crash and some
sort of strengthening joist had obtruded into the passenger cockpit, holding the occupant down as if he
were in a baby's high chair. So I had to hack that
away with a tenon-saw blade I happened to be carrying in the International's tool kit. Then he struggled
out.

Once he was on the ground something of his old confidence seemed to return to him.

'You wish to pursue me? And for what reason, *sahib*?
Is an honest man unable now to take a little ride without
—without——'

The effort had been too much for him. His voice
blurred and faded and he slumped forward in a dead
faint.

'Let's put him in the shade in the back of the truck,' the
pilot said. He helped me dump the inert Rammal in the

International and we put the tailboard up. 'He'll recover there. Is he a crook or something?'

'He hasn't been proved one. But I think the D.O. would like to see him.'

With that lightly-worn ability of the young to clear from the mind anything irrelevant to the moment, the pilot lost interest in Rammal. He'd been just a passenger: he was my concern now. The pilot's immediate worry was doubtless to face an inquisition over the loss of his plane.

'Can you drive me back to Makindu?'

'Of course.'

I made sure the tailboard was securely fastened and off we drove, complete with captive poacher.

'I'd like to hear about the other time you saw a lion attack an aircraft, too. I think you said there was one?'

There had been. It was in the early 'thirties—the time when the greatest revolution ever to overtake hunting was at its height. Till then all tracking had been done on foot, but the automobile made for so much greater speed and the elimination of so many risks that it had obviously come to stay so far as *safari* work was concerned. Not only the automobile but the aeroplane too was introduced as an aid to the hunter of trophies; for the plane could make a thorough reconnaissance of jungle and plain and return to base with a full report on herds of elephant carrying mighty tusks, descriptions of the terrain, dangers to be avoided—all the information the hunter would at one time have had to amass for himself by dangerous investigation on foot. I don't pretend that these new methods ever had my wholehearted approval, but it would be senseless to deny that they speeded things up.

One of the planes used as a 'spotter' over the Serengeti Plain in Tanganyika was piloted by the German air ace

Ernst Udet, who was at that time, I believe, head of the Luftwaffe. With characteristic bravado Udet tried intimidating a lioness and her cubs by swooping down on them in his Fokker plane with the exhaust roaring and the wind singing violently through the struts and wires. But even the roar of the plane did not subdue the lioness's spirit. She roared herself, and her tail lashed furiously as the plane passed overhead. Udet banked and returned, this time deliberately charging the beast. Still she stood her ground, and again he turned, flattened out, and came at her so low that he seemed to be but a few inches from the ground. But this time she had had enough. With a great roaring and lashing she timed her attack precisely at the right moment and as the plane zoomed overhead, clearing her by but a foot or so, she reached angrily up with a great forepaw and ripped at the fuselage.

For a second the plane tipped dangerously sideways; but fortunately the canvas gave way and Udet was able to bring it to rest on the ground without accident. But I don't think he ever tried such a dangerous pastime again.

'I'd never have believed,' I told the pilot, 'that I'd see such a thing happen again. But there you are—life's full of unbelievables.'

He nodded as we bumped back on to the track and turned towards Makindu. 'Me and my hare's foot, for instance.'

'Not so much that. We've all got to have something to believe in.' For a second I harked back in my mind to my foolish belief that the idyllic days at Caerlaverock would never end. They had—irrevocably. 'No; I wasn't thinking of that sort of belief so much as the belief one has in one's own assessments of character. When one's proved wrong it's quite a shock.'

'Such as?'

'Well . . . such as the shock I had when I learnt that the Watutsi——'

'The *what*, for heaven's sake?'

'The Watutsi. They're a tribe who live in Ruanda, and that's a province administered by the Belgians as part of the Congo. It's a mountainous district by Lake Tanganyika.'

As we drove on back to Makindu I told the pilot how I'd discovered the Watutsi to be an extremely aristocratic race of tall, agile warriors who are warriors no longer in the belligerent sense, though for many generations they defended themselves from the weakening revolts that attacked their kingship and maintained an autocracy which seemed to suffer little when subjected to the invasions of Europeans. They are cattle farmers by profession—and indeed could not sensibly be anything else, for the grassy plateaux of the province are ideal for grazing.

The Watutsi are intelligent, law-abiding, and extremely dignified. They dress in white flowing robes not unlike the togas of old Rome, and their care over their personal appearance leads them even to vanity in the manner of their hair styling. I have often seen them sitting for hours at a time while their hair is dressed. In this way they show much the same concern for the result as might European women: but rather more patience.

Another sign of their inner contentment is their way of smoking. Many African tribes smoke, but usually to the accompaniment of hawking and spitting which is most unpleasant. The Watutsi smoke long-stemmed pipes without any such demonstrations of ill breeding, puffing away slowly and gently, ruminating the while and enjoying their mild vice to its full extent.

This pastoral and highly civilized race of people are also unusual in that they neither hunt game animals nor allow their wives and sisters to do menial tasks. Such work is done by a tribe of underlings, the Batwa natives, who might be described as a lower stratum of the same race. It is a tribute to the Watutsi traetment of the Batwa that complete dignity is maintained by both classes. I have never seen any evidence of ill treatment on one side or resentment on the other. There is in fact great charm in the sight of a Watutsi farmer being borne in a hammock by Batwa servants when he goes visiting or shopping.

Their agility is bred and maintained by their natural fondness for sport—high jumping and throwing the cane being the two athletic activities in which they excel and which they practise from childhood. High jumps of up to seven feet are common, and I have often seen these graceful Africans throw a cane two hundred yards with ease. When I mention that other African tribesmen attached to my expeditions could do no better than fifty yards it will be realized that this is a considerable achievement.

They are perfectly content to manage their pastoral affairs efficiently and to live without covetousness or unrest, a proud but peaceful people. This was how I discovered them, and this is still how I like to think of them; but to illustrate my point about assessments of character for the pilot's benefit, I began by telling him how M. Schmidt, the Belgian Administrator of the Province—a helpful and courteous man—had organized a Watutsi display of high jumping and cane throwing for the entertainment of Allan McMartin—whom I've spoken of before—and me. We'd covered some 12,000 miles on our *safari* through Kenya, Tanganyika, Uganda, Congo Belge and Rhodesia in search of game and pictures, and we were most appreciative of both the entertainment and the hospitality. But Allan's love of dangerous sport was so great that when M. Schmidt mentioned that a herd of buffalo had recently been

wrecking the Watutsi farmlands he responded immediately.

'Is it worth organizing a hunt?'

I inferred from the glimmer of amusement in M.
Schmidt's eyes that he had casually mentioned the
depredations of the buffalo with the object of arousing
Allan's interest. 'I think it might be arranged,' he said.

'Don't forget,' I reminded Allan, 'our rifles and
ammunition are under customs seal in Rhodesia.'

M. Schmidt said he thought that was a formality he
might quite easily overcome by his personal representa-
tion to the Rhodesian authorities; and so it was
arranged.

The buffalo were menacing the lives and living of the
Watutsi who inhabited a fairly wide area about six miles
from Kigale, where we were then located.

As soon as Allan and I got ourselves organized—it was
a few days later—we set out. M. Schmidt had arranged
for his assistant to direct us; but for one whole day our
efforts to locate the herd proved fruitless: there wasn't a
single sign that offered contact. We returned to Kigale
disappointed. Then M. Schmidt sent natives out in
several directions, Allan and I following at dawn the
next day. For some reason—perhaps the peculiar sixth
sense of the hunter—we were brimming with hope and
determination this time; and sure enough we had gone
only a few miles when we came to a papyrus swamp
where there were unmistakable signs of a large herd.
The tall green reeds with their delicate umbrella tops
had been trampled into the swamp and shrubs were uprooted everywhere. The spoor rayed outwards from the
swamp in several directions.

We tracked the buffalo slowly and cautiously. Presently we came to some thick undergrowth which clearly
the buffalo had passed through—we could plainly see
the black mud from the swamp smearing the greenery

and the indentations of their hooves in the soggy ground.

M. Schmidt's assistant was obviously very worried about us. He prattled away in Flemish—which we didn't understand—and intensified his gloomy remarks by a pantomime of gestures and eye-rolling which he all too clearly intended us to grasp as a warning that if the buffalo caught us we should be tossed sky-high. This expressive charade only made us more eager to get going, for once Allan's mind was made up there was no budging him.

We entered the jungle, Allan leading, carefully placing our moccasined feet toe first and weight-on-heel, and stopping frequently to listen. The undergrowth was so thick that it needed every bit of skill we possessed to move without sound, for if we disturbed the herd by scent or sound they would stampede.

Our progress was extremely slow. Sometimes it seemed as if whole hours were passing between one soft footfall and the next. Tautened nerves and relaxed muscles have to be achieved in such circumstances; and although I had every faith in Allan's ability I had less in my own—or perhaps pretended I had as a kind of insurance.

As we moved forward with this almost unbearable care the normal sounds of the jungle were all about us: the strange chatterings and shrill calls of birds and beasts who watch and listen and tremble at the approach of man. They might at any moment have disclosed our presence to the evening by their shrieking fear.

Then, after about a hundred yards and what seemed æons of time, Allan halted. We had come to a clearing.

There before us in the glade was a thronged mass of buffalo herded together in their forest retreat, like a vast bovine nation who found safety only in numbers and joy only in depredation.

They saw us at the first movement of the hand that parted the branches. Immediately several of them walked towards us, noses held forward, pressing the air in their suspicion. Clearly they couldn't understand this invasion of their privacy—something which had never happened to them before.

Slowly two bulls advanced a little nearer to us. I saw Allan mount his heavy double-barrelled rifle and fire. It was a perfect left-and-right. The two bulls fell dead and the thuds of their bodies falling, heard above the echo of the rifle, were the beginning of pandemonium.

Menacingly the beasts milled round us. Death, and our presence, terrified and angered them. I was in the very act of reloading my rifle—I had just managed to get one cartridge in and close the breech—when an enraged cow charged us. All the action and movement of the beast were concentrated on revenge. Tail violently lashing and lowered nostrils wide she came at us, and was but a few feet in front of me when she fell dead—killed not by my rifle but by Allan's, whose shooting had been faster than mine and deadly accurate.

After this escape—for which I would willingly, in theory, have stopped to shake Allan by the hand—I was quicker with my shooting. Neither of us was caught unawares again. Within what must have been a very few minutes a barrier of carcasses protected us from the rest of the herd—which were still raging and making a great noise with their bellowings and chargings. We were by now down to six cartridges between us and decided for common sense's sake to retreat and get more ammunition.

We went back to the swamp via the track we had made—noisily but quickly this time. M. Schmidt's assistant watched us refill our cartridge loops and it was clear that he was still regretting his responsibility for our safety.

We returned then to the clearing; but only the dead were there. Now we had to pursue the remainder of the angry beasts.

As we followed the trail showing the direction of the greatest number we scanned every bit of undergrowth which might offer cover. And we were rewarded. Out of clumps of bushes the great beasts crashed in panic. They were so infuriated and ungainly in their fearful movements that there was little chance of getting a decent shot. We had to pursue them from their hideouts much as ferrets would rout rabbits. M. Schmidt's assistant waited for us at a safe distance outside the clearing. From time to time as we went crashing through our orgy of attack I glimpsed his face. It reflected both wrath and incomprehension. Such goings-on were surely mad!

We failed to make further kills that day; but so far as that predatory herd was concerned the Watutsi would have no more to fear for some time. Man, and his gun, had for the time being conquered. The buffalo would now seek a new den—probably many miles away from the one that had proved so vulnerable.

Now as we emerged from the bush and found ourselves at the swamp once more the place was densely thronged with Watutsi. They had heard the sounds of battle and now came to do justice to the abundant slain.

With astonishment Allan and I watched these aristocrats return for a time to the obscene laws of unthinking animals. Buffalo carcasses were dragged from the glade— manhandled to the accompaniment of beastly cries of joy. The long white robes were discarded; smeared with the blood of buffalo and the filth of the swamp they were shredded beneath the feet of wild savages preparing for a carnal feast. The eyes of men who only a few minutes ago had been gentle with rumination and contentment were now frenzied and bloodshot. The Watutsi danced naked round the carcasses of the predatory enemies, ripping and cutting the hot meat with knives and hands, gutting the offal with fiendish delight, cackling with joy as kites spiralled above them and swooped down to join in the maiming of the flesh.

It was almost unbelievable, and Allan and I covered our eyes with our hands, not wishing to witness the degradation of what had seemed to us a noble race; and which is in fact still a noble race. For I could not help thinking that bestiality of this kind is inherent in all of us and manifests itself in different ways in different peoples. But to see it manifest itself in a race so intelligent and highly civilized as the Watutsi is quite shocking.

The pilot nodded. 'Yes. It must have been a bit of a shock. When you come to think of it we're not so far from animal states even in what are supposed to be the most civilized communities. Look what a joy we used to take in public hangings—probably still would if we had the chance. There's quite a kick to be had from the catching of mild law-breakers, too. I daresay you're feeling quite proud of yourself at having laid hands on the Indian customer in the back.'

There I couldn't agree with him wholeheartedly. Rammal had been a nuisance, a mild irritation under my skin; but I had very little interest in the rights and wrongs of the case except insofar as they affected the game he was poaching. And now in any case there was not much to do: the capture was made; I had only to hand him over to the D.C., ring Hardy, and get on with my game ranging.

How easy it all sounded: and how wrong I was!

For when we reached Makindu and I stopped at the D.C.'s office I discovered that Rammal had risked it and jumped off the truck somewhere—though once I'd gained the road my speed had seldom fallen below thirty miles an hour—and had very successfully eluded me once again.

REGARDING ELEPHANTS AND RHINOS

MY own lack of consideration of the possibility of
Rammal's escape from a moving truck had cost me my
captive. Now that I had disproved the fallacy that a
man can't disappear from a thirty-mile-an-hour conveyance I was wiser if not in the best of tempers.

Fallacies concerning game animals have wide circula-
tion too; they seem to become perpetuated in the manner
of old wives' tales. For example, it's often said that
elephants never sleep lying down and that they always
leave guards who don't sleep at all while the herd is
resting. This is no more true than the notion of the
elephants' dying-ground.

I remember hunting elephant in the Makueni district
and coming so close to three bulls—all lying down and
snoring—that if I'd had a postage stamp with me I could
have stuck it on the rump of the nearest one. As it was I
gave him a gentle pat and got no more response out of
him than a twitch of the tail such as he might have given
if a leaf or tick-bird had alighted on him. Such familiarity
when the beast was awake and standing up would be
a very different matter; and as for attempting a pat on
the trunk end—nothing on earth would tempt me.

Elephants are great destroyers of crops and it is their
destructive habits that so often make the hunter kill
them, for their depredations on maize, sisal and other
vegetable plantations ruin the native farmers' economy.
Young bulls are invariably the culprits. They go ram-
paging over farmland pulling down tender shoots from
the upper boughs of trees and trampling everything in
their path. I can remember only one occasion when one

of the destructive herd was a cow. She fell to a shot from my own rifle and when we examined the body we found not only that it was a cow but also pregnant. I had the beast carefully skinned and the fœtus extracted. It was perfectly developed—a young bull—and in my estimation would have been born a week or so later, for its mauve-blue eyes were open and when I persuaded the station-master at Kima to let me weigh it on his scale it tipped 300 pounds. I had the fœtus sent to the Curator of Nairobi Museum.

I suspect that that cow was vindictively destructive because she was pregnant. They begin to breed when they are three-quarters grown and I have often noticed that they are far more dangerous when pregnant than with calf at foot. Once their babies are born they are good mothers and confine their activities to the protective, doing all they can to get the babies to safety rather than leave them for a single moment to turn on their attackers.

The nerve systems of elephants are highly complex and in at least one way produce an effect of fear similar to that in human beings. I remember being particularly reminded of this once when I was elephant shooting in Western Kenya.

At one base I chummed up with a hefty chap who said he also was looking for ivory. We were in fine elephant country; our camp was on a high ridge overlooking a vast area of semi bushland around Berwa, a favoured spot of many fine tuskers, and we had high hopes. Before night fell we'd agreed to divide both the cost of the licences and the spoil between us.

Soon after dawn next morning my native bearer reported that he'd seen three fine bulls moving leisurely across the open bushland towards a lightly wooded gully.

'Our luck's in,' I told my companion.

He took my binoculars and looked through them at

the quarry, still moving with unhurried grace across the plain. He seemed to delay as he handed me the glasses and I noticed that he had paled a little. Then he excused himself, admitting that the elephants had had a purgative effect on him. I may say that this wasn't the first time I'd come across so-called big-game hunters who were reasonably fearless when it came to lions, buffaloes, leopards or rhinos but candidly admitted that elephants always induced fear, with its accompanying embarrassing loosening of the bowel, in them.

But I couldn't afford to wait for him to follow me, for hesitation in any kind of hunting has stultifying results. So off I went with my bearer and we soon entered the gully we'd seen from above and found it comparatively easy to negotiate. In less than an hour I'd accounted for two of the three tuskers and returned to camp. My erstwhile partner seemed staggered by my success and immediately offered to swap his D/B rifle and a cheque for 500 rupees for my .577. This I willingly did and headed back for home that same evening, leaving the man with the over-delicate internal apparatus behind. Nor, having discovered his weakness, was I sorry. For a nervous and highly strung man under the spell of fear gives off a strong odour of sweat which is sensed afar by the quarry, acts like a red rag to a bull and sooner or later turns the beast into an attacker. Calmness and control are at all times absolutely necessary.

Curiously, both the sound and smell of mankind induce fear in the elephant, and that fear is accompanied as in his enemy by loosening of the bowel. I have seen a suspicious beast stand with its great ears thrown forward, trying to catch the faintest sound of snapping twig or brushed leaf, seeming to concentrate more on the vibrations of the ground than on airborne noises. And the moment he hears the tiniest sound to bear out his suspicion that a hunter is near he will turn and be off, his fæces indicating the state of his alarm. But this is only when the hunter is exuding his normal irrepressible bodily smell. The fearful hunter with his sweat ducts betraying his terror is inviting attack, for the elephant—or indeed any killing beast—seems to realize at once that his would-be attacker is in fact trembling with fear and will make an easy victim.

I nearly made an easy victim myself once—not, I'm thankful to say, because of fear or foolishness on my part but because of one of those incidents that crop up in any job and cannot by any means be anticipated. I'm fairly hardened to scrapes of all kinds and have developed a certain amount of what I believe the psychologists call extra-sensory perception; but in this particular case I escaped a charging elephant entirely by luck and not by any skill or judgement on my part.

I was on an ordinary routine job chasing several bull elephants which had been making a nuisance of themselves by raiding native cultivation. The crop in this case was potatoes and they'd developed such a fondness for these that not even a horde of natives yelling war cries throughout the hours of darkness could scare them off. Night after night they came and dug the spuds up with their tusks, consuming hundredweights in a very short time. No farmer could stand such losses and I was called in to shoot the marauders or chase them so far off that they wouldn't return.

The beginning was easy. Together with my bearer I started at sunrise and soon found the heavy imprints of elephants' feet. Dewdrops were shining on the edges of the prints—proof that the raiders had eaten their fill and gone before the break of day. The trail led over the trampled hedges that edged the field and were supposed to keep marauders out, but which in fact were quite useless, since elephants can easily negotiate obstacles up to four feet high.

Red ground squirrels ran ahead of us, conveniently indicating the trail as they made their pickings from the elephants' droppings—which were still tepid, proving that we were not so very far behind our quarry. But this was fairly open country, across which man and beast can move quickly; and I knew that soon we'd come to dense forest—the sort of country where elephants like to rest and ruminate. So I had no illusions about an easy kill. For forested country is the most difficult of all to hunt in—as I was soon to find to my cost.

The trail made a zig-zag course and crossed two streams. Here the banks of rich red earth had given way beneath the elephants' weight. On the far side of the second stream the bush began to get closer; and in a very short time the spoor had led us into dense undergrowth.

Here we paused and began to move forward with the utmost caution, stopping frequently to listen, knowing full well that elephants are both wise and cunning—their cunning having been given them, with their extraordinary olfactory and aural sensitivity, as a compensation for their poor eyesight—and are quite capable of planning an ambush.

At last, during one of these frequent halts, my scout and I heard the sounds we'd been listening for: the snapping of branches as the elephants moved through the forest ahead of us.

We went on, cautiously as ever, knowing that we were overtaking them by the sound of the snapping branches, which now cracked like whiplashes.

What we didn't know at this stage was that not all the elephants had continued the journey. One of them was at that moment settling down to sleep directly in my path, having so far had no whiff of our approach from the down-wind direction.

We moved on unsuspectingly and came to a narrow gap between green saplings. My bearer, more alert and keener-eyed than I was, gave my pullover a tug and pointed to the right of the opening.

There, not more than four yards away, lay an elephant on its side as if dead.

Neither my bearer nor I uttered a sound. This was a moment when only signs could be used to communicate. Peering through the bush I tried to size up my shot. I wanted to aim at the furrow at the back of the neck over the vertebrae; but the beast was lying with his rump towards me and his neck to my left. I would have to skirt the bush I was peering through and move a couple of yards to the left so that I could be sure of a fatal shot first time.

This I began to do; but I had moved only a step when a whiplash sapling, released by my movement, sprang up and hit me on my right cheek and eye.

I must have uttered a mild ejaculation—I don't remember. What I do remember is that my eye started streaming, leaving it quite useless for sighting any rifle, and the elephant, alarmed into wakefulness by my movement, rose up from the ground in fury and began to turn towards me.

From my left eye I had a glimpse of his trunk coming towards me—not clearly, for the greenery, my streaming eye, and the speed at which everything happened made for nothing but confusion—but I knew I had no time to get the butt of my heavy Express rifle to my shoulder, nor could I have aimed it.

My reaction was automatic. Bracing myself, I held the rifle vertically in front of me, pointing upwards at the head of the elephant that by this time had risen and was towering above me, and pressed the front trigger.

The blast of the explosion from the right-hand barrel seemed enormous. I felt it singe my face, and the kick from the unbraced rifle jerked my arm with such momentary agony that I thought it was broken.

But I had succeeded in both frightening and hitting the elephant. There was a sudden great turmoil in the bush, the sound of foliage and saplings being trampled underfoot, and when I peered through the puff of smoke wisping away from the rifle he had turned tail and gone. A stream of blood ran down the hollow between the two rifle barrels on to my hand and arm. My score had evidently been a mere nicking shot, and as a wounded elephant can become more than usually dangerous (besides being in unnecessary pain) I set off in pursuit at once so that I could finish him off. But although I followed the spoor—we reckoned there were two besides the one I'd hit—for the rest of that day we never caught up with them. They were evidently moving fast and furiously through close country. After a few hundred yards there was no longer any sign of blood on the trail, so I think it was fairly safe to assume that the wound had been a very slight one, perhaps just a grazing of the flesh. Anyway, the elephants had had their fright—me too!— and they didn't return to the potato fields again. So my task had been completed to the farmer's satisfaction. All the same, I'd sooner have been sure about what happened to the wounded beast.

A little while after that incident I was able to give the Wakamba natives rather more tangible evidence of my ability.

There was supposed to be a huge old bull in the district, harmless but carrying enormous tusks (their size undoubtedly increased by rumour) which, I was assured, might well make a new record. I have often heard such tales before and am always dubious about their truth until I have the evidence of my own eyes. But in this case the tales were so persistent that I judged the old bull to be at least existent if not outstandingly big.

For a week I hung about the village, which was pleasantly situated on the banks of the Athi river, and enjoyed the peaceful scene. Schools of young elephants paddled and splashed joyfully in the river every day, baboons and monkeys perching in the trees kept up an unceasing chatter, and doves and hornbills cooed and bleated in harmony.

Then my scout brought me news. The old bull had been seen on the far side of the village, tramping his weary way into the close country beyond the river.

I made ready and off we went. Soon we caught up with his trail, but I was disappointed for the footprints were no more than eighteen inches across—not an outstanding size if the tusks were in accord.

However, there seemed to be little doubt about his age. His droppings suggested that his food had not been properly digested. And I was catching up with him, as was obvious from the increasing freshness of the spoor, so clearly he was moving slowly; and as the country here was quite open it was unlikely that he was lingering deliberately: he was old, perhaps a centenarian, and he had travelled many thousands of miles in his long life and now his heart was weary and he could move fast no longer, however open the country.

His trail went on eastwards for some miles, the light breeze in his face keeping my smell from him and perhaps refreshing him as he moved unknowingly towards his elephant Valhalla. But soon he had to rest; and I came upon him quite unexpectedly as he rested in a glade, his body side on towards me, his great tusks supported by a low branch.

They were monster tusks all right, but in poor condition—the tips of both broken off and smoothed round by years of digging for bulbous roots and salt. He found them a great problem in his old age—one could tell that by the awkwardness of the stance he was forced to assume to fit the tusks on to their support—their great weight being too much for his failing heart.

It was a melancholy sight to see him standing there trembling, the hide over his knees thin and withered, the failing strength of an African giant typified in every wrinkle and agueish twitching. He would not last through another rainy season; the stout heart would fail and he would fall in his tracks, his full life over and bereft at last of his immense dignity.

After watching him for a moment I worked round to the left so that I was face to face with him. His great ears picked up the sound of my approach and slowly unfolded towards me. But he was resigned to die and faced me squarely, falling immediately to a simple frontal brain shot.

When I examined him I found that many of his teeth were missing or loose and that those that remained were worn to smooth stumps. This, of course, would account for his poor digestion and lack of nutrition. The tusks weighed 164 and 148 pounds even in their broken condition, and I suppose that the only reason he hadn't been bagged by poachers was the difficulty of getting away with tusks of such great size.

Well, he had fallen now and it was the end of him. My native bearers joyously spread the news of the giant's death (by what means only they know, but it always happens that news is seemingly spread faster through the uncommunicative forests of Africa than over the modern telecommunications of Europe) and within an hour or so natives came in their scores, armed with pangas and home-made knives to divide up the meat they loved.

The Wakamba tribe are not so culturally advanced as the Watutsi, but the fact remains that their orgiastic revels round the carcass are far less horrid in their implications of primitive animalism. The pleasure they take in hacking up the carcass seems to be far more directly concerned with the appeal of the meat as food.

The author.

An elephant can be a formidable, destructive force.

The wreckage of the powerhouse.

The dead culprits.

Full-grown lion dragging his kill to a place where it will be safe from vultures.

Gripped by coil and claw. A most unusual scene in the Masai Reserve, Kenya. An eagle in the coils of a cobra. (Note the clenched grip of the eagle talons, defeating the cobra fangs.)

Python emerging from its home in the sandy gully.

Ostrich, a common sight in East Africa.

Hippo basking.

The beginning of the rhinos' anger.

Colonel Sandy MacNab.

Leopard warning off interlopers.

Vultures feeding while giraffes watch and Kilimanjaro gleams in the background.

The unique albino giraffe photographed by Colonel Sandy MacNab.

Lone buffalo.

Hippo at play in the Athi River.

Crocodile taking in the sun.

Lion feasting.

A spotted hyena making off with a zebra hide—the remains of a lion's meal.

The lion stalks proudly past mildly apprehensive spectators.

It is barbaric, but in a very simple-hearted way and conveys nothing of the degradation of the Watutsi's carnal lusts as they perform their frenzied dance. One can join wholeheartedly in the Wakamba's simple glee.

I watched them as they carved up the carcass, skewering the gory joints on their knives and chattering and crooning away as they reduced one side of the elephant to a skeleton. The larger joints they piled on litters, the smaller they strung about themselves as they prepared to return to their village. None of the meat was eaten, nor was an excessive load carried. Their lack of greed and abstention from bloody rites and offal-eating was entirely admirable. The whole business was conducted with innate decency as well as pleasure.

When the load had been made up the procession of natives started for home. Their infectious laughter sped them on their journey, their mirth exemplified the freedom and joy of their simple lives.

On across the plain and through the woods they marched. Runners sped ahead to warn the village of their approach, and by the time they came in sight of the mud huts with their grass roofs the proper preparations for their reception had all been made.

The women of the village appeared *en masse*, the maidens with a greasy coating over their developing breasts, the married ones naked to the loins and bearing gourds of water for their menfolk to slake their thirsts. Behind them as they came forward in welcome the maidens raised masks—savage but strangely dignified— and banners of red and white beribboned calico—totems to keep off evil spirits.

A little way outside the village men and women mingled and re-formed themselves into a triumphant marching column, now adding music to their joyous shouting—music from curious reed instruments which emitted sounds of martial trumpets and droning noises not unlike bagpipes. Behind the crowd of warriors and women the children joined on, naked, cavorting with their protuberant bellies shaking like those of grotesque dwarfs.

This was only the preparatory festival of welcome. There was a feast in which I was invited to share all they had to offer—their home life, their food of chicken and mealie cobs, and their revelry. The next morning the entire village, from the tiniest baby to the most aged totterer, marched back to where the remains of the fallen elephant lay and cut up the rest of the meat. This was then taken back to the village with even greater evidence of joy and attended with due ceremony as it was cut up into strips to be prepared and dried. In this form— 'biltong'—it would serve the whole village as food for months to come.

The whole ceremony was one which for me typified the simplicity of the Wakamba's approach to life. It is a simplicity which, denuded of its barbaric elements, I have sought and attained and which has brought me happiness and the companionship of Hilda, my wife, and my children. The complications of modern city life in Europe are more than I could bear. Even the noise is too much for me. I remember when I went to London some years ago I stayed at a wonderful hotel in the heart of the West End. Nobody could have had better service, but I simply couldn't get used to the continual grinding of traffic. I made sure that when I went again in 1956 to make arrangements, among other things, for the publication of this book, I stayed with Hilda in a pleasant bed-sitting room in the quiet residential district of Paddington. There I found life bearable. But I could not be happy in any city for long. My nature rebels against the necessary conformity to so many regulations and the lack of active excitement.

The death of that fine elephant reminded me that I have also witnessed elephant births.

I came upon a small herd of elephants one day while I was travelling in fairly open country. From quite a distance I heard fierce screams accompanied by gurglings such as I had not heard before. As I approached the herd I saw the elephants—all cows—gather in a phalanx, facing outward and all looking menacingly towards me. About two hundred yards away stood a solitary bull. Very curious about all this, I got to within a few yards before realizing what was happening. By climbing on to the roof of my truck I was just in time to see that in the middle of the protective phalanx a cow was just completing the act of birth. During her ordeal her protecting matrons of honour continued to scream loudly, as if they too were remembering pain. Immediately the baby was born the mother began massaging and caressing it with her trunk; and within fifteen minutes it was able to stand unsteadily. A few minutes later it was imbibing milk. (An elephant's teats, by the way, are formed with several outlet ducts, rather like a sprinkler.)

By now the music of the attendant cows had changed its note, and I can only suppose that this was a signal to the bull who stood alone like an anxious father in the waiting room of a maternity hospital.

The construction of an elephant's body is, like that of all creatures, miraculous, and I have many times examined hide, muscles and bone construction. The legs, for example, are formed of layers of knuckle-jointed bones and between the many joints are several thicknesses of tough resilient gristle. This cushioning helps to absorb the animal's great weight and minimize jarring while in action, and to walk silently and minimize fatigue.

Inside the body—and so far as I know unique in wild animals—is a container for reserve water. This is always

kept full and from it emergency supplies are drawn when
the elephant is making waterless treks across drought-
riven country or is being sorely tried by the hunter in
relentless pursuit.

The outside, the hide, is engrained with innumerable
wrinkles and folds, and within these the elephant offers
a home to both ticks and lice; but these are kept within
reasonable numerical limits by the tick birds that alight
in dozens on the backs of all parasite-carrying animals
and feed themselves and keep down the insect population at the same time.

As for the brain—I once went to considerable trouble
to ascertain both size and exact location of this organ.

Taking a fine fully developed (but not very old) bull
of good dimensions, which I had killed with a heart shot
to avoid damage to the skull, I had its head dissected and
demolished under my direct supervision by a native
using an axe.

The brain is protected on both sides and at the front
by a hard bony structure. From the rear it is more
vulnerable but the high ridged spine is in itself a protection from the hunter's bullets because it obscures the
aim unless the hunter is in a tree and able to direct his
aim downward directly on to the back of the brain box.

When the top layer of bone was carefully chopped
away it revealed an inner structure of cellular bone, the
cells and pores oozing a rich oily liquid and thick blood.
The native who was doing the chopping, I remember,
called to a number of his fellows at this time, making a
blood-curdling noise of pleasure and gesticulating wildly
down at the head. Immediately natives came running
from all directions and began clamouring for the fatty
chips of bone that flew everywhere as the surgeon
resumed his chopping. These they seized on and sucked
like lollipops.

Fascinated, I watched as the inner bony cellular mass

was demolished, interpolating warnings to take great care so that the brain itself should not be damaged.

When at length the housing had been chipped away the brain appeared as a four-sectioned organism enveloped in a transparent wrapping of skin and tissue. Fibrous nerve centres emerged from underneath and at the sides. These I cut myself with a scalpel, and the brain was removed to be weighed. It was eight pounds and measured 14 ins. by 10 ins. by 6 ins.

The position and size of the brain confirmed my view that direct frontal shots are always the most successful. One can make this frontal shot in two ways: taking aim midway on an imaginary line joining the eyes, or at the base of the tusk—the housing of which is usually five inches across, allowing a fair latitude in the placing of the bullet from a range of, say, twenty-five yards. The tusk shot is the best bet unless one is absolutely certain the beast will not get wind of your presence at the last minute. For if one is aiming between the eyes and the head is suddenly raised in apprehension of your presence the vulnerable point between the eyes is immediately elevated and presents a sloping surface to the bullet, which glances off or, worse, penetrates the trunk; wounding, and probably causing immense pain and anger. The tusk shot, on the other hand, will allow for the sudden lift of the head and still leave a vulnerable area vertically exposed. The bullet entering the tusk area immediately crosses the nasal gap and enters the brain where it joins the vertebrae.

In my heyday I have accounted for sixteen elephants with sixteen consecutive shots—all frontal, either between the eyes or at the tusk base, according to circumstances. But this score is not so remarkable as it may sound, for in every case the elephant was either standing perfectly still, head-on, or moving towards me so slowly that it would have been difficult to fail. I have had many failures in my time too, and these have often been because I have chosen a frontal shot when the beast was moving too quickly. There is no doubt at all that a heart shot is simpler and surer in circumstances when movement or obscured aim is involved.

As to the rifle to be used for elephant shooting, every hunter has his own preference. My own choice nowadays is for the .500 D/B fitted with short 24-inch barrels, made by Messrs. Holland and Holland; but in my time I have owned and used some fine side-lock doubles in the .470 and .475 class. The use of small-bore weapons is less satisfactory—partly because the smaller explosive charge is likely to cause injury rather than death. In any case the existing game laws in Kenya prohibit the killing of large beasts with rifles in the 6.5 and 7 m/m class. It is true that the greatest elephant hunter of all time, M. D. Bell, used light rifles of .256 and .275 calibres; but one has to remember that his skill in placing a shot through the ear or heart of an elephant was far beyond that of the ordinary hunter. Also, in the days when Bell hunted, elephants were unused to the sound of rifle fire and consequently had not acquired the knowledge and wisdom that has since become part of them. By their curiosity and reluctance to move from this strange new creature that had come among them they laid themselves open to attack, and Bell was able to increase his natural skill through practice—over country which in those days was open for endless miles. In circumstances like these the .256 or .275 solid nickel-coated bullets gave excellent penetration. But it would be useless today when one is forced to track beasts into heavy cover and kill them with frontal shots which must be powerful enough to penetrate that great skull and enter the brain.

In tracking, the assistance of the native tracker must be sought. The European is all right so long as he is following plainly defined spoor, but when the tracks fade away on hard ground it is only the keen eye of the native that can detect the signs that are invisible to you and me. Nothing is to be learnt here: it is a natural gift; and when I follow a tracker of the Walungulu or Wakamba tribes as he makes his bare-footed way tirelessly through thorny bush and pathless waste, pausing only occasionally to pull a thorn from the sole of his foot, I am filled with admiration and humility.

Like most African wild animals, elephants are constantly searching for salt. Many of the inland streams have banks in which veins of salt run through the hard clayey earth. It is here that the elephant will dig out the salt strata with his tusks; and when he puts too much strain on a tusk, it will fracture and break off. Often the fracture occurs near the base, where the nerve is lodged, and when this happens suppuration and decay finally form a knobbly and distorted growth. It is a great disappointment to the hunter who has been tracking an elephant whose footprints indicate splendid ivory to discover at the end of the day's trek that the beast has only one tusk. He returns to camp fatigued and gloomy, wishing only that elephants, like rhinos, grew a new tusk after breakage.

Sometimes, of course, the day's trek brings far more ill luck than a broken tusk; one may find disappointment and danger in a much bigger way.

There was a day when, accompanied by a single lithe Masai scout, I sought for giant tuskers in an area thickly populated with elephants.

The method of locating beasts in any given area is a simple one: one finds a hill that gives a good view all round and offers at the same time some cover where one can lie up if observations are likely to be prolonged.

Such a place was easy to find in this area. There was a very convenient hill about two hundred feet high on the summit of which stood many flat slabs of rock leaning again each other *à la* Stonehenge. Here, with the aid of binoculars, I took a good look round.

There were many skeletons and bones of lions and other carnivorous creatures, also countless elephant tracks leading over and around the hill; but for the most part they looked unused and I came to the conclusion—with what an error of judgement!—that few beasts of any kind had crossed or ascended the hill during the recent months and that my best bet was to watch across the bushland below and pick out and track down whatever I saw worth hunting.

For several days we made the summit our headquarters, the Masai sitting astride the highest rock and exercising his superb vision by pointing out with his spear any elephant he thought worth drawing my attention to on the plain below. We made several abortive journeys down the hill but always found when we got there that the beast we pursued was not after all so magnificent in the tusk as he had seemed from above; and since there was no point in shooting merely for the sake of shooting we returned empty handed from these forays again and again.

Then, one afternoon about 5 p.m. we watched a mass gathering of elephants on the plain below. From every gully and hideaway a great exodus began. Beasts of every size and in every stage of youth and decrepitude converged on to the open ground. There were ancient cows with sunken eyes and stumpy tusks and large bulls sporting better ivory than I had seen in a long time. After waiting so long it seemed like the realization of a dream, for not only were the elephants massing and thereby offering us, as it were, a selection parade, but the wind was also in our favour and would allow us to approach undetected until we were quite near.

Metaphorically rubbing my hands I signed to my

scout and we went down—the Masai following behind me with his long-bladed spear.

We had almost reached the foot of the hill when the Masai yelled at me to look behind.

When I turned I saw that a big lanky elephant with broken tusks had emerged from a hideaway screened by a walled gulley and was following us—looking, I may say, extremely malicious, his trunk swaying from side to side as he picked up tufts of grass we had tainted by walking on them and threw them aside in disgust.

This was an occasion when I was not at all willing to shoot. For one thing it was senseless to waste a licence on a tuskless beast, and for another, the sound of the shot would cause a stampeding exodus of the great gathering amongst which I could choose a really worthwhile capture. So we ran off along the track and gained higher ground without bothering about professional dignity. There I shook my Masai scout warmly by the hand. But for his warning that elephant could have approached in complete silence to within a few feet of me and picked me up in his trunk and dashed me to death on the rocky ground. Nor, I feel, would he have had any hesitation in doing so: he was that sort of elephant.

When we looked back we saw that he'd followed us no farther than the spot where we'd run off the track. At that point he paused for a few minutes, still angrily swinging his trunk, then turned off to move purposefully over to join the throng.

There must have been two hundred elephants gathered there and within a few minutes the alarm broadcast by our lanky informer had sent them all into a panic. Screaming and bellowing, trunks raised in fury, the herd broke up into many groups, shouldering each other out of the way and raising great clouds of dust as they stampeded for the many gullies and hideaways they'd come from. They were maddened now with the fear that

spread among them like a disease; their only concern was
to get away—though it could only have been fear of an
uncomprehended danger that alarmed and possessed
them.

There was nothing to be done now. Alarmed as they
were, the elephants were unlikely to mass again. The
scout and I climbed the hill and prepared to spend the
night in our Stonehenge shelter. Next morning we would
return home, our time wasted.

By the time we reached the top the thunderous echoes
of the stampede had died down; the ground was still
again and the dust had settled. Only the ordinary noises
of the African night sounded faintly in our hideout. We
had a small oil lantern and this we lit for comfort as we
settled down for the night.

But there was to be no comfort for us.

About nine o'clock we were awakened by the shrieks
and bellowings of angry elephants. There was no mis-
taking them. And they were coming nearer. In their fury
at our invasion of their reserves they intended to hunt us
out.

Quickly we put the light out. We dared not give the
slightest indication of our presence, they would discover
us quickly enough by scent.

There were no footfalls, only the angry trumpetings
which seemed to be closing in on us from every direction.
Even in the complete darkness elephants, like lions and
other felines, are able to tread their silent way along the
narrowest paths by instinct. We on the other hand, had
to rely on our memory of the terrain at the top of our
hill; and I could only vaguely recall the location of a
cave I remembered seeing fifty or so yards down the
track. If we could find it it might make a safe retreat, for
as I recalled it the entrance was too small to admit an
elephant. On the other hand it could easily be a lion's
den—and occupied at that.

Better try, though. My Masai scout agreed with me and we felt our way from the shelter of the rocks to what seemed by the gritty surface to be the track.

There was a silence now that was more terrifying than the angry trumpetings; for we knew full well that we should hear no sound of the elephants' approach and that some of them had probably closed in on us since last we heard their malicious cries. It was not only possible but highly probable that as we crawled with paralysing slowness down the track we would find our way blocked and suddenly hear the swish of a trunk as it curled down upon us. This was another occasion on which I felt fear— fear at its simplest and most hair-raising because it was partly of the unknown. At what point would my groping hand reach out along the track and touch the great leathery foot that, raised and lowered in the ordinary movement of a footstep, would crush my body to death? How soon now would the angry revenge of the hunting elephants be bellowed a few feet ahead of me?

We moved on—whether in the right direction I had no means of knowing. In the pitch blackness only a vague looming of the rocks could be seen—felt, rather; and my hands, hardened though they were by years of African sun and the gripping of rifle stocks, were bleeding from my fumblings along the gritty path.

Suddenly I felt a waft of dank breath on my face. I froze, my scalp icy, my neck hair rising like quills. There was nothing to do but cling there, waiting for the trunk to encircle me. I could hear my heart thumping and the dripping of drops of sweat from my chest to the ground beneath me.

I said silently in my heart: 'God, give me a break'— such glutinous cringing words, but they were sincere all right.

It was my own fear that was triumphing: it was only a breeze that had touched my face. After an age I realized it. And as if to restore some of my small courage the bellowings of the elephants sounded again—close by, but not, I fancied, near enough for immediate danger.

We moved on. Perhaps a few minutes had passed. It seemed like hours. But if my geographical memory was right we should be nearing the cave.

The bellowings and grunts sounded again. I almost wished for a return of the despairing silence, for the beasts seemed to be on all sides; they had climbed the hill from every direction, knowing by instinct that their encircling movement must in the end defeat us.

There was a downward slope of the ground now, and, as I put out my left hand I felt the beginnings of the wall in which I believed the cave was located.

And now, of course, another fear consumed me : if we ever reached the cave would there be a lion therein? Our utter helplessness was almost more than I could bear. My rifle was worse than useless in the darkness, retreat was cut off in every direction even if I could have seen to make a bolt for it; and there were many hours till dawn.

I rose now and pressed my back against the rocky wall, feeling my way to the left, slowly and carefully. The elephants were very near—that I could tell by the periodic vocal outbursts. Whether we should reach the cave in time, or at all, or, having reached it, find it to be the lair of another enemy . . . it was difficult, even in the midst of my fear, to keep my mind off these questions which seemed to repeat themselves endlessly like a cracked record.

Then quite suddenly as I moved sideways pace by pace my hand detected an inward curving of the rock.

The entrance to the cave !

'Ah!' I murmured to the Masai. It was the first word that had passed between us since we left the summit.

And now. . . .

I felt my way round the inward curve of the entrance. Then I stood and paused. A dank smell pervaded the cavern, heavily oppressive and sinister. And were there rustlings within? I could hear incredibly small whisperings and stirrings, but nothing that sounded as menacing as a lion. The wall was slimy where my hand slid round and something soft and membranous seemed to elude me, to slip away from beneath my fingers with what I felt to be a miniature cry of protest.

I slid round another yard. Still no menace from within. But at the entrance to the cave there was a sudden blocking out of the night: I felt this rather than saw it, for there was scarcely any difference in the tone value of the darkness when viewed from the interior of the cavern.

We had not been a moment too soon: an elephant stood there. And I knew without a doubt that in a second his trunk would reach exploringly inward.

I have seldom moved so quickly. I leapt a good six feet towards the unknown depth of the cave, the Masai moving with equal speed. We tumbled together on to the floor of the cave and there crouched, waiting.

For a long time there were pawings and grapplings at the entrance. We could hear hooves scraping at the surface; and from time to time it seemed that one elephant would move away only for another to take his place and attempt to reach us, bellowing angrily.

But at last there was silence. The entrance was no longer obscured and through it we could see the lesser darkness of the night; and faintly in the distance we heard what we hoped and prayed was the migratory march of the elephants away from our threshold.

For hours we huddled there, not speaking, feeling, from time to time, showers of drips descend upon us from the roof of the cave; but this was a mere nuisance compared with our ordeal of the earlier hours, and we were prepared, having been spared, to possess our souls in patience till the dawn, hoping only that in the meanwhile no homing lion would seek the den.

When at last dawn came we realized that the whirrings and murmurs that had accompanied our terrible waking hours were caused by scores of hairy bats that clung to the roof and had, in their pestilential way, been urinating upon us in showers. Unpleasant, very.

We returned in the morning none the worse—except by frayed nerves—and I had to chalk up a victory to the elephants.

It wasn't the only one by any means. I remember another occasion when I was humiliated and vanquished by a lone beast I met face to face on a track when searching for an apocryphal monster tusker who had been causing trouble among the Makueni women by frightening them while they carried their gourds of water from the stream.

The beast I met was the trouble-maker all right, but his tusks were mere 60- or 70-pounders—exaggerated by the native women into 150-pounders—and once again I wasn't prepared to waste a licence on him.

He, however, was not quite so willing to lose interest in me. He stood directly in my path, fully braced, monumental, his ears forward and his tiny amber eyes with their long lashes watching me and weighing me up as steadily as a cat watches a mouse. There was no more than a fifteen-yard space between us. I was well aware that my safety depended on remaining absolutely still, and I found it extremely difficult; for at such moments one feels an almost irresistible urge to blink or twitch the lips or shift the weight from one foot to the other. That would have been fatal: he would have charged and I should have been forced to raise my rifle and fire.

So there we stood staring each other out. The only movement the elephant made was to waggle his lower jaw from side to side—a movement I took as expressing his contempt. For perhaps four minutes we stood like that; then, as if tired and contemptuous of the whole thing, he allowed his trunk to dangle loosely on the ground, feeling along the surface as if searching for a lost sixpence.

Still I made no move, puzzling out in my mind just what he was up to with that grovelling movement of his trunk. I tumbled to it too late: he was sucking up a multitude of gritty stones. I realized it just as he curled his trunk inward towards his mouth and then with an enormously powerful backhander uncurled it and blew the entire charge of grit and dust over me with great force. I felt the sting on my forehead and face like a charge of buckshot.

Satisfied now with his revenge he gave a last derisive snort, sauntered off the track and continued on his way.

I think the lesson to be drawn from that incident is to remember that when meeting any dangerous beast (except the rhino) *vis-à-vis* and not wishing to kill it the safest plan is to stand still and remain absolutely silent. You may suffer humiliation, but it is doubtful if any worse harm will befall you.

Rhinos are a special problem. Not much sense in trying to stand and stare them out, for if they know you're there they're usually charging you madly. And you want to make sure you shoot them—and shoot to kill—before they get closer than five yards—otherwise the impetus of the charging body (even though the rhino is technically dead) will topple you over and crush you. I have heard people talk of stepping aside from the oncoming bodies of rhinos they have just shot, but have never seen it done.

It is not at all easy to stalk rhinos to their resting places, even if the wind is in the right direction and one is absolutely silent in approaching. They are peculiarly sensitive to the presence of man and appear restless even though they may not be directly aware that you are watching them. Flies, buzzing ahead of the hunter in outrider clouds, are partly responsible for raising the alarm, and there are also the rhino-birds—feathered spies whose mission in life is to utter loud *chir-chir* warning cries as they fly across the bushland and observe dangerous interlopers.

I remember once stalking a trio of rhinos which had been doing considerable harm in a eucalyptus plantation at the foot of the Aberdare mountains, uprooting the trees with their horns and eating the topmost succulent shoots. I'd followed them from their night raid on the plantation to their daytime 'lie-up' in the nearby forest— a basin-shaped hollow surrounded by difficult tall greenery which made vision impossible. I could only follow their trail, foot by foot.

This I did for about an hour, having sent my native bearer home because his footsteps had been far from noiseless and I was very anxious to avoid giving the rhinos ahead of me any warning. Coping with a charging rhino in this thick bush wouldn't be all that easy; I wanted to shoot to kill without them being aware of my presence if possible.

Such wind as there was was in my favour and my approach was absolutely noiseless—that I can swear to. But when I came to the hollow and peered through the tall grass and brush to see the three rhinos lying there in a huddle, rather as pigs do in a sty, I could see that they already knew of my presence. They were beginning to become restless, turning their heads uneasily towards me and preparing to attack. A cloud of flies hovered angrily buzzing above the trio and I remembered hearing the buzzing of flies quite near to me a few minutes earlier. So it may be that flies transmit either a secret warning or bear on themselves the smell of approaching man.

In that particular incident, by the way, the rhinos lost

no time in translating their uneasiness into terms of action. They came charging through the undergrowth straight at me, each trying to get ahead of the others. I fired my .500 D/B Express at the face of the middle attacker. The shot hit her between eye and ear and she dropped dead instantly, her body raising a great cloud of dust as it hit the ground. The other two leapt from the side of their dead companion with the agility of cats— unbelievable in view of their great weight and ponderous bodies—turned and were gone almost before I had time to realize that I was out of danger.

Even though I once carried out the greatest rhino drive of all time—in the Makueni district, to make way for a post-war settlement of Wakamba—I have never ceased to be especially cautious in tracking rhino because of their extra-sensory perception. On only one occasion in my life have I ever got really close to a rhino without his knowledge and that time I was so close that I actually hung my stetson hat on his horn. But he was an oldish bull and he was fast asleep. It was quite an occasion, though; for in a moment or two he detected something wrong, rose fuffing and snorting from his rest and went charging off with the stetson still poised on his horn.

Exit rhino to the sound of gales of laughter—mine and my native bearers', who stood holding their sides and rocking with mirth at the droll sight, even though a moment before they had been warning me—with justifiable horror—not to attempt to do such a mad thing.

MANHUNT VIII

THE ESCAPE

WHEN I reported Rammal's escape to the D.C.'s office I fully expected a big-scale rocket. I knew I deserved it. But nothing like that came my way. It was probably being hoarded for later. At the moment the position with regard to poaching was too serious to consider routine reproaches, and Rammal's activities as set in motion by Hardy and me had arrived at a state which delighted the D.C.

'You've forced his hand, J.A., brought the whole set-up to a convenient head. Just what we want. We only need to capture Rammal to bring the whole outfit to the boil. Then we'll let it boil over. This poaching racket's been going on far too long. Rammal isn't the only operator by a long chalk; but with him out of the way the bottom'll tend to fall out of the organization. A prosecution won't be difficult and with the evidence we've got he'll not escape without punishment. What I'm aiming at is a recommendation for deportation. But in any casè I'll at least be able to justify a bit of spending of government money. The police are handicapped by shortage of staff in the Game Parks, shortage of arms and shortage of waterfront people to keep a closer watch on all those *dhows* that load up secretly in the creeks round the coast. With Rammal sentenced I can convince the Governor that a full scale anti-poaching drive is a necessity. Nearly five thousand pounds of poached ivory in six months: that's what we've traced. It ought to be enough to convince anyone—especially if we've got the king-pin in the lock-up and can confront him with the evidence. Of course, we all know he'll have a convincing explanation for every ounce; but this time the documentary evidence is overpowering. And with you and Hardy as witnesses——' The D.C. pressed his hands firmly on his blotter, palms down: 'Well, we ought to be all right.'

With a good deal of diffidence I pointed out that we hadn't yet got Rammal and at the moment had no idea where to look.

'I've taken care of that as far as I can. Police are patrolling the area, and he can't have got far away.'

'I wouldn't like to say that,' I said. 'He's proved pretty slippery so far. I'd believe anything of Rammal's escaping potentialities.'

'He's not Houdini,' the D.C. said dryly; 'nor the Invisible Man. Nor can he exist any longer than anyone else without food. We've got all his known contacts in Makindu being watched. Working it out logically, where do you think he'd go, and what would he do?'

'If I were him I'd lie low.'

'Exactly. And he's subtle enough to realize that a simple thing like that is the last thing we'll suspect him of planning. He'll be thinking we'll be trying to unearth some complex design, knowing that his mind's oriental and subtle. In this case I'm prepared to bet his subtlety'll lie in his simplicity.'

I nodded. 'A sort of double double-cross.'

'Exactly. So I think it may be a straightforward matter of closing the circle round him. A systematic search of the town and encircling patrols covering a radius of—what?—four miles? That's where you can lend a hand, searching the gullies, the lairs, every spot of cover you can think of. We ought to be able to bring him in within twenty-four hours. Hardy's on his way up and should be here first thing in the morning. I'll leave the planning of

the round-up, so far as the area outside the town's concerned, to you.'

In the morning Hardy returned. He was full of news.
We'd been barking altogether up the wrong tree in
assuming that Rammal had been flying to Mombasa to
reorganize his smuggling plans.

'He's realized the whole thing's too hot for him, that
the evidence has piled up and that he hasn't got a
chance. What he was trying to do was to get away.'

'Leaving his partners in crime in the lurch?' I asked.

'Precisely that. And they suspected as much. Karemchoud was doing the last thing we suspected him of—
blowing the gaff plainly and simply. Apparently all the
hirelings have suspected for a long time that if a show-
down comes they're going to be left properly in the cart.
That was why that shop boy at Voo told us about the
loading of the *dhow* at Mombasa tomorrow. They're
Judases, the lot of them; but we've been working along
the wrong lines in thinking there were wheels within
wheels and double-cross motives whirring them round.'

'Then why did Karemchoud send me that decoy
message?' I wanted to know.

'He didn't: Rammal did. Karemchoud had kept him
supplied with carbons of messages for just such an emergency as this one. He admitted as much to me.'

'Karemchoud? You've got him?'

'You bet. He's a material witness for the Crown. He
knows he's only to turn King's evidence to get off with
little more than a reprimand. Rammal had been black-
mailing him—in what way we don't know; but it'll all
come out at the trial.'

'If we don't get out and get Rammal there won't be
any trial,' I said.

'True. I'm ready when you are.'

We made up two parties, each with a truck, half a
dozen native bearers and a couple of policemen with

sidearms. Noel took the area to the east of Makindu, I went the other side, towards the Chyulu mountains. I don't know why, but I had an idea Rammal might return to the crashed plane. Noel had a notion he might try to make the Athi river where it comes to within about eight miles of the town. There was a chance he might try for some sort of river transport there. Wherever he was and whatever he planned he must know his hours of freedom were numbered. Lack of food and water would be his undoing if nothing else.

Then I had a sudden idea. I asked one of the young policemen if he knew whether private charter planes carried anything in the way of emergency rations. It seemed they did—two persons' food and drink for one week.

At that rate Rammal might well fox us once again. This was something even the D.C. hadn't thought about. I wondered if Rammal would have the sense to lie low during the day and the nerve to move by night. If he had it might even be possible for him to get away from Makindu. But the risks would be pretty great. I remembered with a slight tingling of the spine the night I'd spent in the cave with the elephants pawing at the threshold. And the Chyulu range was full of lions' lairs. Somewhere along that escarpment the lioness with her cubs would have made her home. Perhaps Rammal's outlook wasn't so healthy after all.

AT MY OWN RISK

ONE day in the early 'thirties I was returning to my home in Nairobi when a message was delivered to me.

It was from Hilda. *Glen Kidston wants to meet you and discuss
plans. Lunch New Stanley Hotel Friday.*

I think only the magic of Kidston's name stopped me
from cursing aloud. I had just completed a three-months'
safari in the Masai Reserve and had accounted for eighty
depredatory lions and ten leopards and I was very tired.
Rightly or wrongly I thought I had earned a spell of
rest. But as soon as I saw Kidston's name on the form I
was filled with renewed excitement. He was famed at that
time as the partner of Woolf Barnato the racing driver;
but this was only one facet of his many-sided and adventurous career. A great flyer, he seemed to bear a charmed
life, for he had survived two major plane crashes. And,
as if neither air nor ground held enough adventure for
him, he had also had an outstanding career in the navy,
both on surface ships and as a submarine commander.
I knew, of course, that he enjoyed the pleasures of big
game hunting, but I had never come across him in
person before and now here he was asking to lunch with
me to discuss plans. It was wonderful! I had no feeling of
disappointment at all over my vanished rest. Whatever
Kidston did, I was prepared to swear, it would be
unusual in conception and exciting in execution.

So it proved. Kidston, who was stocky and obviously
immensely strong, also managed to give the impression
of great agility. All his movement as he swung into the
hotel lounge for our coffee after we'd completed lunch
suggested speed and nimbleness. I remember conjuring
up a picture of him shinning up and down the most
complicated ship's rigging. In the African forests it might
easily be an accomplishment that would serve him well.

Kidston's plan was to carry out a big elephant drive in
the area east of Kitui.

'I need practice in those head-on shots, Hunter; and I
think you're the man to show me.'

After shooting some big tuskers—the hinterland east of

Kitui was at that time largely unexplored territory and harboured some of the biggest of Kenya's elephants— Kidston planned a much more unusual *safari*—to the northern frontier district. There, he had heard, there were Greater Kudu of a size unsurpassed by anything in Rowland Ward's Book of Game Records. He'd set his heart on such a bag; but I couldn't help thinking it was the attendant circumstances of the expedition that appealed to him as much as the possibility of acquiring a unique trophy; for the northern frontier district, round Lake Rudolph and Mount Kulal, is inhospitable, wind-blown country, waterless and constantly raided by Abyssinian brigands from over the border.

The elephant *safari* was set in motion by Kidston's determination to get things moving at a much faster rate than seemed possible at that time; for it was in the days when such roads as existed in Wakamba Province were extremely poor. I pointed out that a motor *safari* would inevitably be a thing of slow progress. This wouldn't do for Kidston at all. 'Right,' he said, 'you see to recruiting all the native labour. I'll get things moving on the roads.'

That was literally what he did, for he departed immediately for Nairobi, where he bought an enormous and varied assortment of road-clearing tools. These were all distributed among the natives and their delight knew no bounds when they were told to get cracking on clearing everything in our path. We cleared a continuous stretch of scrub as far as the eye could reach, and as we went the tiny dik-dik antelopes tripped ahead of us as they emerged from the waste we were razing. These tiny creatures have a Disneyesque quality of daintiness and seem to exist entirely without water, obtaining what moisture they need from bush shoots.

After we'd established a base camp for our motor transport and the casual native labour, Kidston and I

struck out into the unknown. We'd gone barely a mile
when I nearly put my foot on a puff adder—I heard it
making its characteristic noise only just in time. This,
our first kill, was looked on by all our native bearers as
an omen of good luck. And indeed our very first day's
trek—a good dozen miles—brought us to a 'donga' or
watercourse which on digging welled up with an abundant supply of palatable water. So we were further
encouraged. Also, the natives in this part of the forest—
most of whom were honey hunters whose pots were hung
in every available hollow tree for the reception of wild
bees—told us that up to now no European had hunted
elephant in the region ahead of us, and they implied
that we should find the finest beasts we had ever seen.
With many awed gestures they told us of monarchs
whose tusks were so huge that they rested on the ground.
We nodded agreeably but without enthusing when we
heard this news, for I had warned Kidston that nearly all
native stories of this kind are wildly exaggerated—not
deliberately but simply because there is a natural desire
to please and encourage the white hunter.

However, the area we finally discovered at the end of
three days' march was in fact noteworthy for the number,
if not the size, of elephants. Kidston delightedly shinned
up tree after tree to get a god-like view of the magnificent
elephant country I'd brought him to. I refrained from
tree climbing personally, the ground seeming the natural
place for my feet, but from time to time I caught glimpses
through the scrub of as fine an elephants' stronghold as
the hunter could wish for.

For another three days we remained there and under
my tuition Kidston mastered the frontal brain shot.
With very little practice he managed to kill, with one
shot apiece, three magnificent bulls, each with hundred-
pounder tusks. Such clean kills would have been the
envy of many a professional hunter.

Although we had so far reached only the fringe of this rich elephant El Dorado, Kidston was satisfied with his progress with the .470 Webley & Scott rifle he'd brought and with his ivory. We returned in triumph to Nairobi to be refitted for our trip to the northern frontier—a venture very dear to my heart because it offered new terrain and experience; besides, I had become infected with Kidston's enthusiasm all the time we'd been on the elephant trek. He had that quality of inspiring enthusiasm in everyone he associated with, and I think this was brought about by his unfailing attention to the needs of others before he considered his own comfort. No native bearer or porter went unattended on Kidston's *safaris*: everyone had the utmost consideration, often at the expense of his personal needs. He was a perfect example of the rich man—and he was pretty well endowed with worldly goods—who had never allowed riches to corrupt him or rob him of his consideration for others.

The first phase of our *safari* brought us to Archer's Post on the Uaso Nyiro stream north of Mount Kenya. From there we had a clear run up the motor road to Laisamis and then on to the administrative town of Marsabit, ninety-five miles due east of the foot of Lake Rudolph.

At Marsabit we went to see the administrative officer, H. B. Sharpe, who had telegraphed back to Cucher's Post while we were there asking us to be sure to call on him as he had some papers he wanted us to sign. Both Kidston and I were completely mystified. As we walked into H.B.'s office we said simultaneously:

'What's all this about signing some papers? Do we have to make wills or something?'

H.B. welcomed us warmly but with an underlying tone of gravity as he said:

'That might be a good idea, too; but the papers I had

in mind *must* be signed before I let you go on your way. They're declarations absolving the government from responsibility should any . . . accident befall you. You're going up to the border area at a time when raiding gangs of Abyssinian and Turkana brigands are becoming involved in an increasing number of skirmishes—some of them pretty unpleasant. It's quite on the cards that you'll be——'

'Say no more,' Kidston said. 'We'll sign, won't we, J.A.?'

'You bet,' I said.

I think at that moment the idea of a scrap in which more unusual occupational hazards were involved appealed to both of us. We'd heard of the border brigands who ride in at dusk on camels, horses and mules, their turbans rakishly set, their bright gowns billowing and the knives in their belts ready for action; but neither of us had, as it were, personal experience. Some of the brigands were said to be armed with rifles and machine guns, which they'd stolen or been mysteriously supplied with. Their object in life was to plunder the border farmers' cattle or attack and rob whatever *safaris* they happened to come upon. The thought of seeing them in action—perhaps even crossing swords with them—added the final touch of spice to a venture we were already looking forward to with what used to be called bated breath.

Kidston and I signed, declaring that we went forward from Marsabit at our own risk and peril. Then we went off to shoot pigeons in a field of H.B.'s oats.

Next day we returned to Laisamis, where, through H.B.'s good offices, we managed to hire some camels. These we should need to transport our kit northward again across the Karoli desert to Mount Kulal. But we had to wait a couple of days for the camels to be assembled and we spent those two days hunting, though not, as it turned out, very profitably. The area is a bleak one, windswept by 'dust devils'—the miniature whirl-winds that twirl upwards like tops throughout the day—and exhibiting nothing but a landscape of the most un-compromising rocks. The few antelopes we saw looked parched and starved. Well worn animal tracks led through the narrowest of defiles to the little water there was and it was plain that many rhinos in their search for water had become wedged between the rocks and had died lingering and painful deaths. In the sparse trees vultures gathered relentlessly and peered with hideous patience on a zone in which only they found profit. All around lay the bleached skulls and bones of rhinos and camels—grim reminders of accounts rendered and debts collected by the carrion.

We camped in this desolate spot and all night a howl-ing wind sounded a ghoulish accompaniment to wakeful-ness. At dawn scavenging hyenas crept close to our camp and intensified the wind's howling with their despairing cries. It was a din that made the blood run cold and the spirit sink.

In the morning our camels arrived and we set off on our *safari* at the earliest possible moment. As soon as we were clear of the place, even though the going was fairly tough, our spirits rose and we had no more anxieties about the wisdom of our plan.

Lake Karoli, in the middle of the Karoli desert, is com-plimentarily but inaccurately named. Rain had not fallen for three years and the lake could best be likened to a car racing track—a shallow and perfectly flat oval ex-tending for many miles. There were just two swampy patches in the area. But in spite of the scarcity of water, the sapless bush and shrivelled foliage, there was a good variety of beasts. In our first day we saw rhinos, oryx, Grant's gazelle and other species of antelope; these, and the numerous geese, duck, and sand-grouse showed no fear of us and in fact paid little attention at all to our presence. The scarcity of water had evidently imbued in them a necessary confidence for normally antagonistic animals were to be seen drinking together among the straggling reeds at the water's edge. The young native girls, however, whose task it was to water the domestic stock, were quite clearly terrified of us. They had never seen white men before and their abject fear as they cringed away from us, dribbling and even wetting themselves uncontrollably, was pitiful. But they learned to accept us in a few hours when they saw that we meant them no harm.

Beside the watering places we found several rhino hides, twisted by the blistering heat. Some of them were perforated by machine gun bullets and we surmised the Abyssinian raiders had recently crossed the border. Only the horns had been taken; evidently ivory was not their current objective, for rhino horns are of little value. It may be that they needed a supply of battle trumpets.

The place was so parched and the atmosphere so lethargic that we came upon rhinos sound asleep at eight in the morning, no tick birds having given the beasts advance warning of our presence. But we left them alone, having noted that the only remarkable thing about them was that their horns curved forward instead of being set erect or curving slightly backwards. We also came on the pug marks of lions. But there was no clue to the presence of the Greater Kudu; nor had we really expected to find one nearer than Mount Kulal. We were really marking time and hoping to get a glimpse of the raiding brigands. But Kidston shot two splendid oryx—the best I have ever seen, with long scimitar horns that rippled in the morning sun.

Several nights passed uneventfully. Then came the night when we were all awakened from sleep by a distant trembling of the earth that grew louder and louder.

Immediately the entire camp was awake. We could hear our natives going into paroxysms of throat-clearing and coughing—their usual reaction to approaching danger.

As the galloping hooves of the raiders came nearer, Kidston and I looked at each other without comment. Our *safari* lamp must have been visible for miles. We judged it fairly certain that the brigands would attack us if only for the sake of our camels. We went round the camp rallying the natives to some semblance of defence; but we had little success. The brigands were riding from the east and the drumming of their horses' hooves had become by now a thunderous tattoo.

We saw them riding down the skyline towards us. Their yells and hornblasts were wild in the thin parched air and the dust rising from the clattering hooves rose like a mist around them. Their cloaks were flying out and as they got to a point no more than a hundred yards distant they vanished into a depression which had once been a small lake. Their cries were muffled then and Kidston and I braced ourselves for an attack, suddenly and rather terrifyingly aware that there were at least a score of them and that they were almost certainly armed with machine guns as well as more primitive weapons.

It was a grim moment as we waited for them to ride over the crest. The natives behind us were in several kinds of panic, for they knew full well that the raiders' night vision was extremely good. They had heard—as we had—of the dreadful mutilations that were part of the skirmishes, and had little faith in their ability to beat off heavily armed warriors.

But for some reason which we shall never know an anti-climax concluded this incident. While in the valley the raiders, either intentionally, or under the impression that our numbers and capabilities were far greater than they actually were, changed their direction. The thunder

of their ride went on, but in a moment we saw them
climb the side of the valley away to our left. And like a
legion of wild huntsmen they were gone from sight, the
thunder of their passing leaving the earth trembling long
after they had vanished in the blackness of the night.
Kidston and I returned to bed quite satisfied that our
contact with the brigands had been theoretical rather
than actual.

In the morning Kidston and I continued our journey
to Mount Kulal on foot, leaving the camels to carry the
equipment. Although these animals undoubtedly have
their uses I find them abominably smelly and uncomfortable as a method of personal conveyance. They kick
and bite on every possible occasion and scream wildly
whenever their drivers try to tether them. Their lack of
co-operation is only bearable because of their ability to
cope with big loads in country where no other beast of
burden would be of use. Personally I was quite happy
for the soles of my boots to wear right through in conse-
quence of the rough going—as they did—rather than
suffer the olfactory and muscular horrors of camel
transport.

As we drew nearer Mount Kufal the terrain became
more rocky and dangerous. Fissures constantly appeared
in our path and we were forced to increase our distances
by seeking ways round which invariably led only to
deeper and wider gulfs.

But as if in consolation we saw many Klipspringer
antelopes—charming creatures which always seemed to
be in groups of two and three springing lightly from rock
to rock with unerring accuracy and immense *joie de vivre*,
their habits and appearance very similar to those of the
chamois. A curious thing I noticed about these little
creatures was that in this frontier district both males
and females carried horns; yet in Uganda the females
were hornless.

We arrived at last at Mount Kulal and I must say I found it a great relief to rest once more; though I am quite sure a camel would have given me no more comfort on the long journey across the desert.

On our left when we camped that night we could see Lake Rudolph away to the west; its turbulent waters with splendid white-crested, billowing waves a wonderful contrast to the endless surrounding landscape of volcanic rocks. I strolled a short distance towards the lake and to my great delight almost immediately identified the spoor of Greater Kudu—two or three sets of footprints being clearly visible. This raised our hopes considerably and we planned to make an early start in the morning. But before going to bed we carefully set by an emergency water supply, filling four-gallon cans which we then buried in the sandy bed of a stream. This supply we intended for the journey to our next camp near the foot-hills of the Matthews range some eighty miles to the south, for there was little likelihood of plentiful water supplies *en route*.

Our plans for an early start were set awry in the morning. As soon as we ventured outside the tents we found that Mount Kulal was thickly enveloped in fog. Swirling white banks of it moved like quiet wraiths across the landscape. The ghosts passed and we could hear the sound of the lake's lashing waters. Then they marched again in muffling silence and we could hear nothing but a faint murmur as of a mountain stream. So it continued for an hour or more. We decided to wait no longer but take our chance.

Kidston wisely took his .470 D/B, reasoning that a single-barrelled gun would be difficult to aim in the fog, whereas if a chance of a shot offered with the D/B in his hand he could use it like a shotgun and have a better chance of accurate placing. I did the same and we moved off together into the gloom, stepping cautiously and

hoping that the swirling fog would thin out as the sun
rose.

We had gone about three hundred yards when a large
form loomed up directly ahead of us. For a moment I
thought it was a buffalo, and as we were within easy
charging range I nudged Kidston. He immediately
raised his heavy D/B and fired—a single shot which
dropped the beast. I was mistaken, but happily so: the
beast which had looked so vast in the fog was the very
one we sought—a splendidly horned Greater Kudu.

Kidston was delighted. Providence had surely arranged the foggy meeting and he could now return
triumphant. The beast itself was in poor condition, with
a previous bullet mark on its shoulder where some
Abyssinian poacher had attempted a kill—no doubt to
get the horns for use as a battle trumpet; but this was of
little account. The horns were in any case the only
valuable part and these were in alpha-plus condition.
There and then we summoned up natives and had the
trophies removed. Then we continued with our hunt.
The fog had not lifted, but in spite of this we hunted
throughout the day and Kidston managed to bag a fine
buffalo. I was beginning to realize that the fog, far from
being a deterrent, was in many ways helpful, for it
deadened the senses of animals and our reactions on
coming face to face with them were invariably quicker
than theirs. I recalled how when I was a lad shooting
geese on the Galway flats I always had a good bag on
foggy days because the birds were forced to fly low and
were slow to correct their mistakes in direction and so
often came exactly the way I wanted them to fly.

Our trip so far had been well worthwhile: the oryx
and kudu alone were valuable; but one of Kidston's
objectives had been to cut a landing strip in Turkana
country near the Matthews range, for he planned to return
again by aeroplane and use the landing strip as a base to

operate from. So after we'd hunted a little more without coming on anything more interesting than a rhino that ran away as soon as it saw us, we began to reassemble our kit for the journey south.

When I went down to the stream to collect our emergency supplies of water I had a shock. The cans I had so carefully buried in the sandy bed were gone—stolen, we could only suppose, by Abyssinian border brigands, though our native porters had seen nothing. It was a mystery that was never solved. Our concern was not so much over the water, for there seemed to be a storm brewing, and in any case the stream would replenish our supply. But the thieves had taken the cans as well as the water and we had no other spare containers of any kind. There was nothing to do but make the journey relying on our basic supplies.

That night the storm broke. It was localized over the Lake. Not even a spot of rain touched us in our camp in the foothills. We went a few hundred feet up the mountain and watched the enormous onslaught it made on the already turbulent waters. Breakers of mountainous size rose and exploded while rain fell in solid glistening sheets and barbs of lightning bore down and struck at the very depths of the turmoil. I had never seen anything like this seething fury of the elements—which resembled nothing so much as an apocalypse in miniature, and perhaps not even very miniature. Steam, mist, hail, fog, thunder and a minor earthquake seemed to combine in working out the destiny of some volcanic dervish. We could feel the mountain we stood on shiver at its very heart with the subterranean rumblings that had their outlet only a mile or so away. It was terrifying; and the fact that we ourselves stood watching from an evening of comparative calm—there was nothing abnormal about the weather on the foot of Mount Kulal except a high wind—increased rather than diminished the scare.

On we went next morning and by the grace of God managed to complete our journey to Matthews range without delay, so that our water supplies held out. In fact we found water we had not expected—of a soupy and brackish kind—at an elephant hole. Elephants are the dowsers of the big game creatures. They can detect the presence of water up to a depth of two hundred feet to my certain knowledge, for I once watched several of them stand over an unopened borehole which showed no sign of surface water whatever while their trunks wriggled and stretched with all the sensitivity of divining rods.

The country where we now camped in the foothills of the Matthews range was much cooler and in every way more pleasant than the Karoli area. This was the land of the Turkana. These savage and war-loving people soon sent representatives to us to see if we had any meat to give them. They are obsessive flesh-eaters and will do anything to increase their supplies. This, I told Kidston, was where we negotiated for labour for the construction of his airstrip. 'Splendid,' he said. I told the Turkana that I would keep them supplied with all the zebra meat they could consume if they would clear bush and scrub and level off the ground for us. Their eyes glistened. They went off to consult with the rest of the tribe and later returned agreeing with our proposals. The men looked very fierce with the circular razor-sharp knives fastened to their wrists, while the women, who were entirely naked except for a belt of jangling shells hanging round the belly, wore a defensive spike piercing the upper lip which would have taken the heart out of any suitor who tried to be too familiar.

They were dubious at first of our promises, but I had seen that the country was well populated with zebra and rhino and that there wouldn't be much difficulty about maintaining supplies. Nor was there. And although the

Turkana were reluctant at first even to let us take their photographs they couldn't do enough to please us as soon as they saw the endless supplies of meat we kept bringing in. Soon we had the whole village—men, women and children—all joining in the task of clearing a dense undergrowth of acacia and thorn for Kidston's airstrip. Kidston had arranged for his mechanic, Neal, to join us and while the natives cleared the ground Neal and I removed the demolished scrub in motor lorries. Every now and again Kidston would go off and shoot a zebra to sustain the Turkana. The quantity of meat they consumed was amazing. I saw women gorging until their bellies were distended and bloated and their bodies bloodied with their continual attachment to slabs of raw meat and dripping entrails. But it seemed to make no difference at all to their capacity for work.

The airstrip was completed in a few days and we could then once more give our attention to hunting. Neal said he'd like to accompany us, and he came on one occasion; but it was an unhappy experience for him because he was taken by surprise by a rhino which charged him from behind and forced him to take refuge in a wait-a-bit thorn—the double-hooked type of thorn bush from which it is impossible to extricate oneself without damage. Neal was very tattered and torn by the time Kidston and I released him and showed a gloomy reluctance to accompany us again.

That same rhino, robbed of his target, took his revenge on us by invading our camp kitchen and spiked Kidston's specially made canteen on his horns. This rubber-lined wooden box contained all our best china and cutlery and we were afterwards forced to fall back on the chipped enamelware that Kidston hated. The rhino's revenge was most effective. In point of fact I could have prevented it by shooting the beast, for I arrived in the kitchen at the operative moment; but it is an unwritten

rule that the man who is financing the *safari* has the
privilege of shooting everything. I would have been
justified in shooting only in self-defence. Kidston—or
anyone else in his position—would rightly have sacked
me on the spot for wasting his licence unnecessarily. So
although he was mad about the loss of the canteen he
attached no blame to me and merely cursed the rhino
for venting its spite on us when it had the whole of
Africa to wreak havoc on.

The following day there was an incident with consequences that were almost disastrous.

Kidston climbed a tree and said he could see a great
assembly of vultures, probably indicating a lion's kill
and by implication a lion. We did a circular tour up-
wind and surprised a lion which did not spot us until we
were fifty or so yards away. It made angrily for the cover
offered by some bush quite near us and before entering
the bush stopped and faced Kidston, who fired his .318.
The lion went down, thudding to the ground as if for
keeps. We started towards the body, but suddenly it rose
and made off at full speed. Evidently the bullet had only
passed through the tissue in the shoulder area. We
tracked the lion for a long way and were rapidly gaining
ground on it when it decided it had had enough of being
pursued. It turned suddenly, right in our path, and came
for Kidston with truly alarming speed and menace. He
fired at once and hit the lion in the mouth, breaking a
jaw bone, and this put it down temporarily, while
another shot finished it off completely. But it was a nasty
moment—one that went to prove that absolute accuracy
of aim is essential.

I remember a similar incident experienced by Cowie
and Bowker, both fine hunters of the old days. They had
gone up to the Maru river area of Masailand and were
in pursuit of a heavily maned lion which had slunk away
and turned to face them just before entering scrub cover.

Immediately Cowie fired at its head and the lion slumped lifelessly to the ground. Cowie walked up to claim his prize: but just as he was within touching distance of it the lion leapt to its feet and was on top of him. He was knocked flat by the enraged beast, which stood over him with its blood soaking his clothes. Bowker came to his aid at once and dispatched the lion with a bullet at point-blank range. The first bullet had fractured the lower jaw and there seems little doubt that but for that fact the lion would have seized Cowie and mauled him beyond hope.

Kidston's *vis-à-vis* with the wounded lion was really the only untoward incident of that whole fine *safari* to the northern frontier territory. We had come unscathed through the hazards of awful warning, which had proved to be far less hazardous than we expected, we had built an airstrip for future reference, and Kidston could now bear home in triumph the trophies he had sought and found. We returned now to Nairobi and the trophies were duly admired, mounted, and shipped back to England. Kidston had a last drink with me before he sailed for home.

'It was a damn' fine trip, J.A. I want you to plan another, just as unusual, and we'll go shooting again next time I come over. Meanwhile, I want to get in a bit of flying, cut the record time between Jo'burg and London. It ought to be quite possible. Right?'

'Right,' I said. 'Till next time then.'

'I'll be back.'

He went and a little while later the news of his record flying time on the journey from London to Johannesburg was broadcast to the world. But it was his last journey, his last *safari* into adventure. His plane crashed in the Drakensberg mountains and his charmed life was ended. So he did not come back.

His solicitors wrote me saying that it would have been his wish that I should be paid the fee for the *safari* he had asked me to plan. He had never, they added, let anyone down in life and they enclosed a cheque with their compliments and remained mine faithfully. . . .

MANHUNT IX

THE SIEGE

WE drove out to the crashed aircraft and searched the wreckage. I had been right: there was no sign of any emergency rations. The container had been forced open. Rammal had been sharp on the uptake.

'All right,' I said. 'The only thing's a systematic search.'

Slowly we covered every inch of the ground on the north-east corner of the Chyulu range. There were footprints in the dust round the wreckage but they faded out on the rock and it was a devil of a job picking them up again. Rammal had the advantage of time and the wind obliterating his traces. Nevertheless, my native boys picked up signs of spoor along the sandy bank of a stream. Evidently he'd passed this way.

By this time we were coming to the escarpment. We searched three caverns in the rocky face of the earth without success. I had the truck brought up and we began a new area of search. Nothing. An old lion eyed us scornfully from a distance and made off. I watched his progress and saw that he made for a lair perhaps a quarter of a mile higher up the escarpment. I made a mental note that Rammal was unlikely to be in that one for long if he'd chosen it as a refuge. But no signs of royal anger drifted down to me.

As I came out of one of the deep fissures of rock a baby warthog dashed out almost from under my feet and scuttled off. It was a reddish brown specimen and may have weighed ten pounds. I had a glimpse of the horrid face with the embryonic tubercles projecting upwards from the snout and the piggish eyes. The long thin hair quivered all along the neck and back and the creature looked ludicrously ugly as it scuttled away on its short legs. I wondered what had caused its nervousness, for it was obviously already in retreat when I almost stumbled over it and I could see no source of danger. Warthogs invariably live in holes dug by other animals—wriggling themselves in backwards—and I watched to see where it would go.

I was wrong about there being no source of danger: the warthog's enemy was above. I heard now a great beating of wings and looked up to see a splendid martial eagle bearing down on the hog, which was now uttering clearly audible grunts of terror. It had reached its hole and was grotesquely reversing into cover. But too late. The eagle made a final swoop at frightening speed and seized the hog by the neck with its talons. Wrenching it from the burrow with a couple of beats of its splendid wings it took off with the hog squealing but held in a vicelike grip. It rose about a hundred feet into the air and suddenly let the hog drop with a thud to the rocks below. Immediately there was another downward swoop, a seizing of the inert body and another ascent and release. Again and again the eagle dashed the body of the shattered hog to the rocks, swooping down to catch it again almost as it thudded on the ground. Then it bore off finally with its prize and soared away towards its eyrie somewhere at the top of the Chyulu range.

It wasn't the first time I had seen an eagle in action as closely as that. The Makindu and Kiboko areas are favourite preying grounds of both the martial and tawny kinds, and only a week or two before I had seen an attack on the burrow of a family of six woolly bat-eared foxes. The eagle had seized one of the babies in a relentless grip and was trying to peck its eyes out, but the little fellow was putting up a fine defence by biting the bird's

leg with its sharp little teeth, and as I approached nearer
with the intention of giving some assistance I saw that
the eagle was feeling the pain its tiny opponent was in-
flicting and was having to release its own grip. Two of
my scouts rushed forward enthusiastically and beat at the
eagle with their hands. It clumsily tried to attack everything at once, found that impossible, and beat a hasty
retreat. The little fox bolted down its hole for dear life;
but I can't think that it was in particularly good shape
by then.

From where I stood now I watched the eagle soaring
away out of sight, the warthog a tiny speck between the
talons. Farther up the escarpment the two policemen
and the bearers were proceeding with the search. I too
now joined them. Cave after cave we found to be un-
occupied, even by the lions we half expected. But at the
end of three hours' search we had a clue. One of the
bearers had picked up Rammal's footprints again. They
appeared on a sandy defile leading upwards to a level
altogether higher than we'd explored as yet. They disappeared again quickly, my boy said, because there was
only a scattering of sand along the narrow path and
soon it gave way to the imperishable surface of rock. But
even there there was some evidence—tufts of grass
bruised as if by the passage of feet, a shrub with a scrap
of cloth adhering to it. But we could not see as yet where
the path led to. It curved away round a wedge of rock
and presumably ended at some lair. I went on up alone
with one of the policemen, telling the others to continue
their search at the junction of the defile and the ground
that was so far incompletely covered.

My companion and I rounded the corner of the wedge
—the path shrank to inches in width just here and we
had to cling on by faith more than balance, carefully
avoiding looking over our shoulders at the steep drop of
a hundred feet or so to the rocky plateau. But we were

round at last and saw quite thankfully that the path widened again and led fairly straight ahead to a blank wall of rock in which there was a conspicuous cave.

I felt quite a glow of excitement. 'Hiding out in there,' I said to the policeman, who smilingly nodded, having come to the same conclusion without my assistance.

We went on. The policeman kept his hand on his pistol. I carried my rifle warily. With a man like Rammal one never quite knew what to be expecting. All the same, there's no denying that I hadn't the slightest expectation of what did in fact happen. It just hadn't entered our calculations.

We were within about twenty yards of the entrance of the cave when a shot went winging over our heads and a spurt of flame stabbed out from the shadowed entrance.

Both of us stopped in our tracks. After the immediate astonishment cooled the reaction was to begin shooting back. In fact the policeman already had his gun out and I'd certainly got my rifle more than halfway to my shoulder. But caution intervened. I gripped my companion's elbow and lowered my rifle. Some thought was needed here. It didn't take long to realize that we'd been manœuvred with diabolical cunning into a position of extreme vulnerability. We couldn't return effective fire because Rammal had the protection of the cave. There was absolutely no cover where we now stood. There was only the one approach to the cave—along the defile and round the wedge of rock. Only one man at a time could negotiate that corner. Given enough ammunition Rammal could have picked off an army one by one. He commanded a strategic position that could be weakened only by his lack of food or ammunition. Obviously he couldn't go on for ever, but he'd cunningly realized that we wouldn't be prepared to risk the lives of men finding out just how long he was fitted up for siege.

Having sized up the position I saw that we were in no

immediate danger. As long as we approached no closer he wouldn't be likely to waste ammunition on us. The one shot had been the warning. Now it was up to us to retreat in humility and work out just what was to be done. I could imagine him—cunning devil—rehearsing in his mind just the time it would take us to return to the D.C.'s office with our news.

We retreated—though not before I'd spent several minutes on sizing up the possibilities of getting at the cave by any other way of approach. It didn't take long: there wasn't any other way. The cave was in a wall of rock which ended sheer, without any circuitous defile, five or six yards beyond the entrance. Above, the rock sloped smoothly back, a dome which merged into the greater heights of the mountains. Approach might in theory have been possible from the other side of the range, which rose to about three thousand feet at this point: but the likelihood of this succeeding without a full-scale mountaineering party was remote indeed. In any case it could only have achieved death or injury, since its object would be to get Rammal to emerge from the cave to give his attention to attack from the new direction while we, from the spot where we now stood, shot him up.

In time, of course, the problem would produce its own solution: Rammal would starve himself out. But we wanted a live and kicking body for trial for poaching, not a dead one for a coroner's inquest; nor did we want dead natives or policemen who had been picked off in malice born of the last stages of despair.

Well, the thing to do now was to report. I wondered whether I should leave a man posted at the defile. It was Rammal's only means of escape as well as our only means of approach; and he might conceivably try to get away under cover of darkness, though I reasoned that for the time being at any rate his impregnable position was likely to appeal to him more than the risk of an insecure future. However, I wasn't prepared to take any more chances with Rammal. I decided to send the policemen and the natives back to the D.C.'s office with the full story and establish myself on guard at the defile. He might attempt a getaway. If he did I should be ready for him.

NIGHT ON THE MOUNTAIN

I EASED myself carefully forward round the wedge to the edge of the defile and peered over. The men were just boarding the truck. It looked quite small, and as it bumped away over the plateau it left with me a feeling of solitude more intense than I had ever known. Although my enemy was separated from me by no more than twenty yards and a wedge-shaped wall of rock, any action on his part, though it would have been welcome, was unlikely, and I was virtually alone in a wilderness of rock and sparse wind-wrenched scrub with mountains rising above me and a hundred-foot drop to the plateau, and the road home, below. Whatever the D.C.'s instructions—whether he wanted the guard continued or whether he had plans for forcing Rammal out with smoke- or tear-gas bombs, it would be at least a couple of hours before any word could reach me. By that time night would have fallen. I didn't particularly relish the prospect, since I had only my rifle as a protection against whatever might choose to attack me, man or beast, and darkness is not the best time to aim a rifle. However, there was nothing to be done; I lit my pipe and settled comfortably down with my back against the warm rock. Doubtless it would be a boring wait; but there were always excitements to recall if not, for the moment, to experience.

There was, for instance, a pretty girl who once begged to be allowed to see what animals came by night to gorge on a carcass. The girl—I'll call her Betty, it suits her, but it wasn't her name—was married very young and the *safari* with her husband was part of the honeymoon. I had been engaged to guide the *safari* and it had turned out to be a very successful one. Betty, for all her very feminine qualities and her insistence on wearing only the very briefest of shorts and a checked shirt, and leaving her shapely legs to suffer the scratches of countless thorns, was a fine shot. In the early stages of the *safari* she got a fine bull elephant and when I told her that the whole great carcass would be disposed of in a very short time by the carnivores of the forest she said she'd very much like to see and hear this happening.

'I don't know about seeing it,' I told her, 'because much of it will be done by night. But you'd hear some quite revolting animal noises.'

'Let's arrange it,' she said with the lusty enthusiasm of nineteen years.

So I arranged to have a thorn enclosure built a short distance from where the dead elephant lay. Within that protective palisade we could watch without harm and if we got the native cook to prepare us some food we could make a picnic of the occasion. This was all laid on and Betty and I set out accompanied by a couple of native bearers—her husband having decided against coming with us.

We were installed in our enclosure by nightfall. It was a perfectly still night, cool and full of stars, but the air was already burdened with the smell of gases slowly escaping through the bullet holes in the elephant's hide. The smell had attracted jackals and hyenas and the wailing cries of a mob of these scavengers sounded eerie

in the stillness. They came nearer and very soon we were
able to peer through the thorn screen and see them
attack the carcass with gusto, tearing at the thick hide
with their powerful jaws but finding it too thick even for
their ravenous efforts. Meanwhile, there was added to
this unseemly din the grunts of approaching lions. The
scavengers, aware of the fact that they no longer stood
any chance, made a last frantic scrabble at the carcass
and then slunk off, guffawing and pretending indifference.

We watched as five lions converged on the carcass and
tried in their turn to rip it open. But it was inflated by
gases to a great obscene mountain of smooth tight hide,
and as they leapt upon it with claws fully extended they
could do no more than inflict weals on the surface and
tumble ignominiously to the ground like kittens. This
went on for some time. The lions became more angry at
their failure every minute and their growls grew to full-
scale roars which made the ground reverberate.

Betty now began to complain of pains in her stomach—
not caused by nervousness or fear but more probably by
some warm soup which we had brought in a thermos and
which I had thought tasted a bit sour when we had tried
it earlier in the evening. It was, she said, essential that
she leave the room for a while, lions or no lions. I
escorted her through the thorn door, stood guard and
returned with her to our refuge in due course. The
beasts who saw us made no attempt to attack or even to
show much interest. They were far too interested in the
elephant carcass to bother with us. But by the time we
returned their persistent attack had successfully torn
away the hide at the most vulnerable part of the abdo-
men and suddenly there was a great explosion of pent-
up gases which released the stench in all its suffocating
horror. It was as much as I could do to bear it myself,
and as for poor Betty—in her already nauseated state she

would have been completely justified in fainting. But—all honour to a veritable triumph of mind over matter—she didn't. But clearly I had to take some kind of action. I said, 'Let's get the hell out of here, even if we have to sleep out till dawn.'

She and the bearers agreed and we beat a hasty and rather undignified retreat. Aided by the light of my small pocket torch and the flashes of lightning in the southern sky we made camp within the hour. So much for our picnic occasion. I never again tried carcass-gazing by night, and I certainly wouldn't advise anyone else to do it. Once is enough for some experiments.

For some reason the recollection of Betty led me along a train of thought to another married couple who once engaged me on *safari*. This blue-blooded pair were a Prince of the house of Schwarzenberg and his wife—a Princess in her own right. His Highness was a real sportsman and the Princess a splendidly proud creature whose bearing was in no way demeaned by the scanty garb she wore—shorts even briefer than Betty's and blouses of finest silk. These two lived in elegance even in the heart of the Masailand bush; but milady's boudoir was always set up at some distance from her husband's sleeping tent. From my own tent I had a complete view of the area between, and I remember that one night I lay puffing at my pipe before retiring when I saw His Highness emerge in a long and elaborately befrilled nightgown and stroll across to the boudoir. In a few minutes he emerged again and came over to my tent.

'You don't stay long,' I ventured.

Gloomily he said, 'Nothing but a peck on the nose tonight. What a life.'

He sat down beside me on the bed, his nightgown ballooning out, and began telling me stories. They were graded progressively bluer and before long we were vying with each other in club smoking room stories of the bawdiest kind. In the morning the Princess remarked:

'Hunter, you must have heard good tales last night. It sounded like a taproom. Perhaps next time I might join you?'

Her irony was not wasted on me. I suspect her husband got a drubbing and was told to behave in a more princely way.

With them, I think the *safari* was solely in aid of sport and pleasure—as it should be; but quite often I have been professionally engaged by people who seem to be seeking relief for pent-up emotions and past tragedies and who believe that Africa, with its paradoxically populous solitude, can give it to them.

There was, for instance, Leonora, who came to Kenya on a photographic *safari*. She was a handsome girl who had a look of haughty indifference about her and she arrived at the New Stanley Hotel, Nairobi, one day about noon. An hour later I walked into the lounge to meet her, having been summoned by a peremptory telephone call, and found her wearing a theatrical outfit of cowboy chaps, checked shirt and neckerchief, high-heeled spurred boots and a six-shooter cuddled on the brass-decorated belt on her thigh. Strangely, there seemed nothing at all incongruous about this get-up. She picked up a 16 m/m ciné camera and various other bits of photographic equipment from the sofa and slung them about herself. 'Let's go,' she said.

I was, as they say, nonplussed. 'It isn't quite as easy as that, Countess,' I said.

'We arranged it all, didn't we?'

It was, of course, true that all the details of the *safari* had been arranged in advance. I had known that the Countess was recovering from an illness and that ciné photography was her one relaxation and that she wanted a grand tour that would bring the widest possible variety of animals within camera range. But no one can summon all the personnel of a *safari* out of thin air at a moment's notice. Nor did I think she'd be very happy stepping through the bush in high-heeled boots and sheepskin chaps. It was, after all, around ninety degrees in the shade most of the time. I think she sensed by my demeanour that I wouldn't be very co-operative towards such a scatterbrained project as our immediate departure. We sat down together on the sofa and I explained to her that I'd be quite ready by the following morning. I also gave her sundry bits of advice about wearing clothes that would be really comfortable. I suppose I sounded very much like a dutch uncle. Her nervousness immediately took on an aggressive form again.

'I'll wear what I damn' well like,' she said.

I wanted to remind her that I considered myself responsible for her safety, but I refrained, shrugged instead and repeated that all would be ready for her the following morning. I had a notion that she was either a very temperamental, or a very sick woman. Her green eyes and wide firm mouth were superbly arrogant, but something about her bearing betrayed insecurity and fear.

The following morning we started off as planned. Leonora had defiantly retained her cowboy garb—presumably as a gesture—but I noticed that she now wore soft leather heelless shoes. I passed no remarks.

Our first day's hunting was a great success. Animals seemed naturally to present themselves for photographing. Some of the finest specimens of lions, elephants, cheetahs and buffaloes I had seen for a long time crossed our very tracks or were induced to turn round and face the camera. It was all most gratifying and at the end of the day the Countess looked a hundred per cent better in both health and temper.

We camped that night and had our evening meal round a small fire. I had supposed she might want to hear some of my *safari* tales, but I naturally waited for an invitation to begin. None came. I sat there puffing at my pipe with the Countess reclining on a kind of *chaise-longue* made of canvas and bamboo. And quite suddenly she began to tell me about her early life in Austria. She had been an actress, and as she spoke of those days in a voice which by some strange alchemy evoked all the elaborate sophistry of lives lived out beyond a proscenium, I lived within a scintillating world curiously compounded of fustian and poverty. I can make no attempt to repeat the details of her story. I am not sure that many clearly emerged. It was a build-up, a sum-total, which she presented to me. Through it all I could hear the stage-hands' mockery, the producer's tantrums, lines from plays that were wholly unfamiliar to me, declamations, curtain speeches, the buzz of conversation. And I could see the glitter of diamonds and the sheen of silk under the shaded lights and the magnificent expanse of velvet curtain swinging down and down and down again upon the footlights.

At a performance given by royal command she had been watched from a box by the Earl of S——. He attended on her in her dressing-room after the final curtain like a suitor in a Victorian melodrama, plighted his troth there and then and presented her with five dozen red roses.

As she told me this her head turned towards me and she said with a wonderful expression of recollected astonishment:

'Now, Hunter, tell me—where in hell did he get five dozen roses at that time of night?'

It was a beautifully timed line, and, having said it, she simply rose and sauntered over to her tent, leaving me warmly amused.

This, as I learned during the next few days, was typical of Leonora when she was on the heights; but her moods of black despair were quite frequent, bore no relation at all to the day's successes or failures, and could descend upon her as suddenly as a breeze. In many ways she made a trying companion, since I could go to endless trouble to seek some specially photogenic group of animals only to be told in no uncertain terms to go to the devil. Needless to say, she alienated herself completely from the natives, who, like a good many white people, understand consistent behaviour but are completely foxed by sudden and complete change of attitude.

During her more amiable moments I learned that her marriage to the Earl had continued as melodramatically as it began. He treated her, I gathered, with relentless possessiveness—typical, I should guess, of his misunderstanding of her mercurial character. Things went from bad to worse. Reacting against his jealousy she indulged in mild flirtations with other men. One of these developed seriously and the inevitable climax was upon her almost before she knew it. Her husband, acting true to type, followed her to her lover's flat and discovered them in a passionate embrace. Thereupon he flicked a revolver from beneath his evening dress cloak and shot the young man through the heart. Having done this he fired one more shot into his own brain and fell at her feet. It was so theatrical a story that I began to suspect her of flights of her own histrionic imagination; but she carried the newspaper clippings of the reports of the case in a little gold chain handbag and, anticipating my incredulity, handed them to me with an air of small triumph.

Even as I read them her mood changed. 'The bastards,' she kept muttering: 'oh, the bastards.' When I handed the clippings back her face was tearstained and ugly and I noticed that she had fallen back into a habit she had of picking at the skin and cuticle around her finger-nails, leaving them raw and bleeding a little. Clearly she was in a neurotic state, and although I could understand the wisdom of her doctors in advising her to take a *safari* holiday I wasn't at all sure that it was doing her much good. But at least her sudden attacks of despair had aroused a lot of sympathy in me and I could only hope that an ear lent to her outbursts and an appreciation of her happier moments were at least relieving her of a lot of emotion which might have remained pent up with dangerous results.

But as things fell out there very nearly was a disastrous outcome to my efforts to help her.

We were cruising along in the truck one day when I noticed that she had slumped down in the seat beside me as if with abandonment to utter weariness. Only a moment before she had been leaning enthusiastically from the cab with her camera at eye level photographing a herd of fat little zebras trotting away across the plain. Now she pushed the blond hair back from her cheek and began to weep uncontrollably.

I longed for something interesting to distract her attention, for I felt that the way to treat her was as one might treat an inexplicably unhappy child. And as luck would have it we had only gone another mile or so when we came upon two rhinos meandering along the track towards us with the calm and dignified mien of two old gentlemen out for a walk. They kept perfectly in step and might almost have been said to be smiling with the sycophantic smiles of local bigwigs meeting a distinguished visitor.

Mood or no mood, this seemed to me too good a chance to miss. I stopped the truck and nudged Leonora. At the same moment my bearer nudged me and pointed to the right where a group of lions had posed themselves exactly as in one of those Victorian family portraits, with a fine black-maned lion and a lioness squatting behind a trio of recumbent youngsters—all of them eyeing us with great interest.

'Look,' I whispered, 'you'll never get two pictures like that again.'

Without saying anything Leonora got out. She began to walk straight towards the two strolling rhinos. They stopped and eyed her suspiciously. Her chance of filming them in motion had now passed. I thought she was crazy—she could quite easily have leaned out of the cab and taken the pictures without moving from her seat. I couldn't think what the devil she was up to, since I had always found her extremely able as a camera technician.

Then, as I watched the rhinos' suspicion turn into active dislike as she approached them, I realized that this time I had not succeeded in distracting her attention from her own gloom; rather, she had seen in the opportunity a way out. She was running towards the rhinos waving her arms in deliberate provocation, and her hysterical crying had risen to wild screams. She was attempting suicide before my eyes.

It was a nasty moment. I grabbed my rifle and ran after her. In a moment or two the rhinos might work their anger up and charge. From the corner of my eye I saw that the lions too were far from happy; they had begun to prowl around with tails lashing and jaws working in a most disturbing way. But my immediate objective was Leonora.

She had covered a good twenty yards by now and I knew perfectly well I could never reach her by the time the rhinos' patience became exhausted. And once they began their charge I should be unable to shoot because Leonora would be directly in the line of fire. There was only one chance and I took it. I stopped and fired two rounds into the air in the forlorn hope that the noise might disturb them enough to deflect their purpose.

Curiously enough it was Leonora's purpose which was deflected. At the sound of the shots she stopped almost as if one of the bullets had hit her and turned to face me, her face working with fury and anguish. Then she began to run towards me, screaming all the profanity and obscenity of the hysterical neurotic's released emotions. I caught her in my arms and with an enormous effort—she seemed to have the strength of a madman and was clawing and beating at my eyes and neck—managed to force her to the ground. Having done this I held her there by brute force. It was most ungallant, but very necessary.

Now I saw—praise be—that my blind firing into the air, coupled with the alarming scuffle with Leonora, had in fact had the effect I'd intended. The rhinos were making off. The lions watched for a few more moments while Leonora's screams continued; then they too turned and wandered away.

I now only had Leonora to deal with—and heaven knows she was problem enough. But after a while I began to sense that sheer exhaustion was overcoming her. Her screams diminished to sobbing cries alternating with wild laughter and her body began to relax. I began to distinguish coherent sentences and gathered that she was haranguing me for having spoilt her attempt at suicide. She had nothing to live for and she hated me for robbing her of the chance of death.

I listened as calmly as possible to all this and when I judged she had pretty well exhausted her hysterical fit I picked her up and took her to the truck. There I laid her on an improvised bed of canvas sheeting and watched over her until she fell into a sleep of utter exhaustion. Then I drove her as carefully as possible back to Nairobi. We were some fifty miles distant and the journey, at the speed I judged safe, took three hours. Arrived there, I had her taken to her bed in the hotel and a doctor was summoned. I explained everything to him and he gave her a sedative. 'It may be,' he said, 'that the worst is now over. *Safari* life and all its interests may win in the end.'

He proved to be right. After that horrifying day Leonora seemed for some time to be very subdued and still not very happy. But she continued her photographic *safari* with satisfying results so far as her mental health was concerned. But, alas, she'd lost those two pictures for ever; and she'd given me the fright of my life— unless that dubious honour could be claimed by the night I came downstairs in our Makindu house without bothering to light a torch.

I had heard some small sound and, thinking the screen door had not been bolted properly, came down to investigate. I found the door loose, bolted it, and decided to go into the kitchen to get a drink of lemon squash. There was bright moonlight, but in the kitchen I needed a torch to find the right bottle. There was one kept on the table and I put out my hand for it; but instead of the wooden surface of the table my hand touched a soft, thick mass of *movement.*

Whatever it was was alive and crawling, and when with some nervous muscular reaction I pressed down- ward my hand only sank into the yielding mass of . . . what was it? I pressed harder and felt a stickiness clam- ming my fingers. These were some small live things that I was crushing.

I had a fleeting memory of a story I had once read— D. K. Broster's *Couching At The Door*—in which a man is haunted by a small, spider-like manifestation, a scrap of fur. I felt myself trembling violently with horror, and all the time the soft creeping absorbed my fingers. I was quite certain now that if I withdrew my hand the creep- ing would come too. Yet for all that I forced it to move around, search for the torch. Surely it should be in just this very spot on the table? It was too big to miss—one of those handlamps of the simplest design, in which a heavy square dry battery is held in a simple metal frame with a bulb and reflector on one side. I had some sort of crazy

notion that it was there in skeleton form—the frame laid
waste with the block battery eaten away. Surely, amid
this writhing stickiness, this illimitable creeping, I could
feel the empty frame?

And suddenly it dawned on me that these were soldier
ants—those termites which march in columns across
Africa devouring everything in their path—their numbers so great that they can strip paths through forests and
houses alike, leaving no scrap of living or edible matter
in their wake.

Now that I knew my enemy I could deal with him.
Fire is the only weapon one can use against this pest and
I was forced to hold my hand and arm in the flame of an
Aladdin which I hurriedly lit—a bit of scorching being
preferable to having the flesh eaten from my bones.
That done, I forced the ants to deviate from their course
through my kitchen with the aid of red hot branding
irons heated in the stove. I hadn't seen such a formidable
column of ants since I'd visited Lunga-Lunga, a small
trading centre near Kwale in the southern tip of Kenya.
There, they had been in continual evidence along with
several other pestilential disturbances including vicious
scorpions, centipedes in endless variety, hairy tarantulas
and clouds of mosquitoes rising from the swampy paddy
fields. Lunga-Lunga had little to commend it except the
presence of sable antelopes—the sable being one of
Africa's most beautiful creatures.

As I sat there on a ledge of rock awaiting instructions
from the D.C. I began to feel sleepy. I wouldn't let myself
sleep, for an enemy lay only a few yards from me; but I
thought there was little likelihood of his attempting escape
since his only possible exit was round the defile, which I
was watching and which would reveal him as a completely vulnerable target. He would almost certainly
guess that someone had been left on guard and he'd be a
fool if he risked making sure. Rammal was no fool, so I

guessed he'd stay put. I puffed away at my pipe, hoping the smoke would drift round the corner and by sight or smell confirm my presence. And I let my thoughts drift into those fragmentary memories which seem so right at dusk.

There was Nganda—Nganda of the Wakamba who came to me as a *safari* cook, bearing references which implied that as a cook he was a wonderful can-opener but that as a tracker or bearer he showed much promise, having come from a long line of great bow-and-arrow hunters. I smiled at the irony and looked at his stocky body and good hands.

'All right,' I told him, 'you'll cook for me.'

His reference couldn't have been more accurate: can-opening was his métier. But always after returning from hunts he would watch me cleaning my rifles and in time begged me to explain the workings to him. This I did and his interest in guns developed to such an extent that he began asking me to teach him to shoot. I took time and trouble over him and very soon he became a cracking good shot as well as a wonderful tracker. My wife was the first to remark on the strength and thickness of his legs—'it's a sure sign of stubbornness, I doubt if he'll give much ground to you or anyone else.' I found that judgement to be very true, just one more example of Hilda's shrewdness in judging character. In fact, on one occasion Nganda proved so stubborn that he almost lost his life.

I had always impressed on him the advantage of getting as close as possible to one's quarry, so one day when he was tracking a raiding bull elephant into the densest part of the Makueni forest he increased his speed until he was but a few feet behind the beast. Here the growth of foliage and thorn was so dense that even with the trampling of the elephant's feet and the passage of its body there still remained monstrous tangles that sprang and fell and trailed across the path between Nganda and his quarry. For this reason it was not surprising that the elephant, turning now in real anger to face his pursuer, was suddenly towering above him and about to beat him to the ground with a mighty downward swing of the trunk. There was no time for Nganda to raise his rifle to his shoulder and take aim. But neither would he give ground or run away. The elephant's mouth was wide open and the trunk already raised for the death-dealing swing down. Nganda was aware only of the cavernous throat and the angry bellow that was showering him with saliva. But without hesitation he took exactly the right action—his only chance. He thrust the rifle into the elephant's mouth and pulled the trigger.

Immediately the elephant staggered back. The shot had entered the brain through the palate. There was a stinking whiff of acrid smoke and an instantaneous contraction of the huge jaws. The rifle was torn from Nganda's hands and clutched tightly in the jaws of the toppling beast. Only as the great body fell with an earth-shaking thud to the ground was the weapon released—bloody now, and twisted out of shape by the death grip.

Stubborn as ever, Nganda had refused to turn and fly even in the face of death; and had brought off a kill that must be unique in hunting history.

We discovered afterwards, incidentally, that that particular elephant had 'gone musth' as we call it when sexual desire induces frenzied attacks on stock, crops and human beings. When I inspected the carcass I found the usual evidence of this condition: an oily and pungent secretion which had escaped from glands on either side of the head and permeated the furrowed hide. Once this happens the elephant invariably turns into a rogue.

Nganda, by the way, is still with me, and though too old now for excessively violent activities is nevertheless still sound in wind and limb.

Another odd and rather charming character I recall

from my early days in Africa was Costa, the Goanese trader. This was when I was hunting the Elemborasha area of Masailand. I was the only European in this lonely area. There wasn't another within fifty miles; and during the rainy season, when watercourses flooded over I was marooned for weeks at a time and dependent entirely on game birds and my shotgun for food. But I knew that as soon as the floods subsided enough to leave the single dirt track negotiable once more Costa would come.

His route was from a tiny trading centre in the foot-hills of Kilimanjaro to Kajiado, some 150 miles north-west, and he travelled in an ancient motor vehicle which was held together with string, safety-pins and bent nails and had wheels of slightly different sizes, so that its progress along the track was eccentric to say the least of it, and produced such a clatter of loose merchandise that all the game for miles around ran in terror. He carried no weapon of any kind: he was a staunch Catholic and all his faith was placed in a well-worn Bible which he carried in his pocket and would brandish furiously at any animal that dared to look at him. Usually, as I say, they ran madly before the onslaught of his transport.

At that time I had a gramophone and a dog for company. Costa always asked me to play some of my many Harry Lauder records to him, and while they were playing he used to sit cross-legged, his Bible clasped in one hand and the other raised in a Buddha-like blessing on me, my music and the pleasure he got from it all. Incidentally, when I was playing the gramophone on my own at night all lion noises ceased. However much the beasts had been growling and grunting, as soon as I put on *Roamin' In The Gloamin'* or one of the old Scottish lullabies there would be no more lion disturbances. My dog, on the other hand, would wail like a banshee. Life, alas, is an imperfect thing: 'never the time and the place and the loved one altogether.'

MANHUNT X

THE ATTACK

It was dawn before anyone came—understandably, since it was unlikely that any plan of campaign could have been formulated before then. I slept a little, uneasily and with a chill creeping through my limbs. At last the policemen and the natives returned. I imagined Rammal watching the truck approach, making sure his gun was loaded, perhaps even considering attempting some pot shots at the men as they made their way up the mountain to me. But I didn't consider he'd give that course of action much thought: it was altogether too risky, he'd have had to come right up to the defile to draw a bead on them.

The D.C.'s message was that he was above all reluctant to cause any bloodshed; even flesh wounds and minor injuries to anyone were to be avoided if at all possible. It wasn't just the apprehension of a poacher he had to consider: moral and political problems were involved and there would be far less sympathy for Rammal if we caught him without violence, and, if possible, without starving him into submission. He invited me now to go down, have some food and sleep and then go and see him. Meanwhile the police and bearers would set up camp and arrange a proper guard.

I agreed with this decision wholeheartedly and after the truck had been unloaded of its rations and camping equipment for the party I drove back to the town. There I luxuriated in a bath, ate a good meal and went to bed.

It was afternoon when I went into the D.C.'s office. 'I daren't put a foot wrong now,' he told me. 'With Rammal in the bag the poaching racket will be virtually at an end. There's a whole team of men—including a survey aircraft pilot—completely organized in a surreptitious way and ready to go into action as soon as this prosecution's under way. Surprise raids will be made on those little offices in Mombasa's back streets where all the business is done; the plane can do all the necessary patrols and watch for dead or dying elephants that will clue us up as to poachers' locations; and there'll be legislation passed to give the right to stop and search *dhows* at sea. But the slightest personal malice towards Rammal will give members of the poaching racket a leg to stand on—and believe me, they're adept at twisting irrelevant circumstances round to suit their own book, whether it's by delaying action or by securing an acquittal on grounds of racial prejudice or unfair treatment. So there's the position: I don't want a single man of mine lost or injured, and I don't want Rammal injured—or starved out either, if it can possibly be avoided. Now: got any notions?'

'Tear gas?' I suggested.

He gave me a half smile. 'Actually I hadn't forgotten that one. But there aren't any tear-gas bombs in the place. The police stores had some chloracetophenones for quelling civil disturbances, but they've been stored wrong and are useless. Anything else?'

'Wait a bit,' I said, 'how about improvising one? I had a sudden thought that Jacob at the hospital might help. If he's got any kind of chemical that makes the eyes smart we can put some in a corked glass bottle and——'

'By God, J.A., you've got something there! Hold on a tick, I'll do some telephoning.'

Jacob the African dresser and virtual chief medico at the hospital was busy—attending a confinement as it happened—but his dispenser, Claude, an equally intelligent and charming African, was helpful. He'd have to look up, he said, just what the lachrymators were. Could he ring us back? We waited twenty minutes, drumming our fingernails on the D.C.'s desk, and both of us sprang for the phone together when it rang.

'I can obtain you a concoction approximating to ethyl iodoacetate with great pleasure and little delay. In a thin phial it will burst like a bomb. But someone, sir, will please have to collect. There is no message boy at the moment in residence. You could perhaps, sir, do that?'

'No perhaps about it. Mr. Hunter'll be up in a truck. And congratulations on your resourcefulness. You're sure it'll be effective without harming the eyes?'

'Effective, sir, yes—as I know to my dismay. The streams are still running from my eyes. But I think it will pass by in a few minutes away from the concentration. I will expect Mr. Hunter, then, with pleasure.'

Claude had put the mixture in a tightly stoppered blue poison bottle neatly labelled 'The lachrymator, not to be taken, dangerous on release into the air.' I added my thanks to the D.C.'s and assured him that his ingenuity would not be overlooked.

He smiled warmly. 'It is all, sir, a part of the Austin Reed service'—a phrase he must have recalled from his training days in London.

I drove now at a good lick out of the town. The bottle-bomb was safely packed in wadding in the glove compartment in the dashboard. I had, at that moment, no real notion of how the bomb was going to be thrown effectively. I suddenly realized that the D.C. almost certainly had expected me to return and discuss my plans with him. But I decided it was too late now; and anyway no one could make foolproof plans in advance for such an attack on such a stronghold. Circumstances would order the method to be used.

Crossing the main road I caught sight of two dark splotches a half-mile or so to the south. Although I

couldn't really afford any delay I justified my detour—
to myself anyway—on the ground that whatever it was I
could see in the distance might be something relevant to
the matter in hand.

It wasn't. But it was a sad sight. Two magnificent
cheetahs—a dog and a bitch—had been struck and
mangled by some careless fast-driving tyrant of a driver.
Not only that: the bitch had been carrying a litter of four
pups and the shock and injury had resulted in what must
have been an agonizing abortion. It was pretty clear
that the driver had made no attempt to swerve, but,
rather, had driven straight at the poor beasts as they
came towards him down the highway, confused and
hypnotized by the dazzling lights. The fast and dangerous traffic of Africa's main highways is something
which animals have not yet learned to cope with.
Felines, bull buffaloes and elephants are inclined to
tramp for miles down the easy surface and hundreds of
deaths are caused every year by carelessness or deliberate
brutality on the part of motorists who choose this wicked
and cowardly way of purposely killing or injuring
animals. It may be that these wretches think there is
justification for killing the dangerous game beasts—
lions, rhinos and the like—by any method at all and that
there is a brilliant triumph to be gained from driving a
two- or three-ton vehicle at thirty or more miles an hour
at a confused and defenceless beast whose nature is
normally savage. But the cruelty does not rest at attacking savage beasts with the equivalent of battering rams.
The smaller, harmless and charming creatures are no
more exempt from careless or brutal drivers than are the
felines and pachyderms. I have many times found the
maimed bodies of serval, civet and genet cats, white-
tailed mongooses and the very beautiful and quite innocent bat-eared fox, all squashed to pulp by the wheels of
cars or kicked casually to the side of the road for vultures

to pick at. Such unnecessary destruction never fails to arouse my fury.

Perhaps because my anger was now welling up in me I felt even more anxious to get back to the mountain attack. I had begun to turn the truck round when I realized that I needn't go all the way back up the road: there was a short cut across country, with a convenient path through a thicket which would bring me right on to the westward track to Chyulu. It was heavy going and I had to follow a zig-zag course to avoid the many rocks and patches of thorn and scrub; but through the thicket and beyond, I knew, the going was easier.

I took my time, forcing myself to calm down, ease my blood pressure, and save the springs of the truck. The thicket loomed up ahead of me—a forest bower perhaps half a mile square with sandy paths and animal tracks criss-crossing between dense bushes of thorn and willow. Here there would be shade from the burning afternoon sun, and I'd probably save five minutes on the run.

Congratulating myself on this minor bit of cleverness I entered the thicket. Almost immediately the ground sloped downward into a pan-shaped hollow with a tiny stream crossing the bottom. I'd forgotten the stream; but it offered no real obstacle, it was scarcely more than a trickle, certainly not deep enough to get bogged down in.

I accelerated a bit as I went down the slope and crossed the stream with hardly a splash. Beyond, the path twisted upwards between acacias and dense thorn; and it was as I rounded a bend that I saw the rhinos— four of them huddled together like hippos directly in my path, glaring at me angrily.

I stopped the truck and got down. Any other time rhinos would have ambled off at the sight of a truck. These, however, decided to stand their ground. They continued to glare at me as I got out of the vehicle. Then two of them got up and lumbered off into the bush. The other two puffed and snorted, then rose and moved belligerently towards me. I didn't like the look of them at all—especially as I was now standing between them and the truck, which was blocking my own escape route.

The leading rhino—a large cow with particularly long horns—now decided to charge. She came at me pell-mell, head down. At about fifteen yards I fired the right-hand barrel of my D/B .500 and she collapsed dead. Instantly the bull followed, came to the dead body of his mate and attempted to jump over it. At the same time the two beasts that had wandered off emerged from the bush—I could see them out of the corner of my eye, tossing their heads angrily at the smell of death and preparing an attack. But there was no time to consider them. The charging bull had already clambered over the obstructing body and was coming for me. The sandy dust rose in a cloud, obscuring my vision; but without aiming properly I scored a lucky shot between the eye and the base of the ear and the beast toppled over sideways. The remaining two rhinos were altogether beyond me. They were coming for me diagonally, both chambers of my rifle were empty and there was no time to reload. I made a hopeless effort at opening the breech, but by then they were on top of me. The whole of Africa seemed at that moment confined to the narrow space between the trees of a thicket—a small world filled with pandemonium, dust, dappling sunlight and fear.

No: perhaps not fear on this occasion. There was really no time to be fearful and nothing to do except hurl myself sideways on to the dead body of the bull rhino, which by its impetus had skidded almost to my feet, and cling on to its horn as I sprawled across the great head and neck.

The two charging beasts now collided sideways as they met on precisely the spot where I'd been standing a second before. The thud of their collision made the earth shake. One of them was so winded that I caught the great wheezing blast of breath he snorted out. It was exactly like human halitosis smelt through an olfactory amplifier. If I hadn't been pretty well knocked out by my strategical tumble I might have felt like swooning with the overpowering stench.

But this was no occasion for swooning. The two rhinos had winded each other to such an extent that they were bewildered and in trying to regain their balance and turn to meet their mutual enemy—me—one of them fell ponderously on to its side while the other was again knocked off its balance and fell too. For a few seconds there was a whirling mass of legs, flanks and horns, a great bellowing and violent scattering of dust and clods of earth and bits of foliage. Once the whirling beasts lashed out so close to me that I felt a sickening thud on the neck of the dead rhino against whose head I was crouched. I took advantage of the turmoil to risk grabbing at my rifle, which had fallen a few feet away as I leapt out of the path of the charging beasts. In doing so I left myself totally unprotected, for I had to leave the shelter of the dead body and dive almost into the middle of the mêlée. But I got hold of it somehow and loaded it just as the two rhinos regained their balance. As luck would have it, their confusion was now so great that they went charging through the thicket away from me. I stood for a few minutes with my rifle at the ready, watching the screen of dust settle and hearing the great bodies trampling murderously through the bush.

Well, I was out of immediate danger—incidentally one of the trickiest bits of immediate danger I'd ever been in —but my path through the wood was now inconveniently blocked by the bodies of the two dead rhinos. There was no room to turn the truck; my only course was to reverse all the way back along the path and out of the wood, then to regain the road and start all over again. This I did, slowly and with considerable apprehension, for I was both trying to guide the truck along a four-foot wide twisting path by reference to the view in the driving mirror and at the same time half expecting to have to deal with the two angry beasts which might at any moment decide to come charging out of the bush. Nothing spectacular happened, however. The only delay was when I got the truck jammed between two trees and had to get out and use a matchet to free the mudguard. I even managed to cross the little stream in reverse without getting stuck. But just as I'd completed that rather tricky bit of driving and was well up the slope on the farther side I saw to my amazement that yet another rhino had stepped from the bush and was blocking my path.

This time I paused only a second to think. There was no point at all in shooting the beast where it stood, since I should then have the path blocked at both ends with bodies of dead rhinos and would be unable to get the truck out at all. My only hope was to get the rhino out of the way by threat or noise. I have often found that rhinos will dash off if they hear the sound of a police whistle; and this I now tried, blowing shrill blasts with all the power of my lungs.

The rhino continued to stand there, eyeing me truculently the while he contemptuously let fall a great steaming heap of excrement which he immediately began to scatter with his hind legs, as a dog does. But he wouldn't budge even when I'd blown myself nearly blue in the face. Obstinate and moody as all his race, he had simply decided to stand there and challenge me.

Well, if whistle-blowing wouldn't move him perhaps the threat of impact would. I let in the clutch and accelerated. The engine roared because of the low reverse gear. I was trying to dodge trees and speed up at the same time. But even the threat of being charged by a heavy truck wouldn't move my enemy. In fact, at the moment when I was perhaps thirty yards from him he decided that the best method of defence was attack, took a few final kicks at the ground beneath his back legs, and came charging down the path towards me.

This is it, I thought, the truck's going to be a pretty wreck after he's gone to work on it. Even so, I still wouldn't risk a shot at him—I suppose because there was always a chance that he'd change direction at the last minute, whereas if I killed him he couldn't fall anywhere but in my path.

He didn't change direction, though: he came full tilt in a cloud of dust until we couldn't have been more than ten yards apart. Then both he and I skidded to a standstill. I could see his great head rearing and snorting as the dust cleared. Then he came ponderously on towards the back of the truck. I thought he'd realized he was defeated and might now crash off into the bush; but oh no! of course he wasn't defeated, and of course he was as obstinate as ever. But he had a sense of humour. I watched him stroll up to the tailboard, lower his head and lift the back of the lorry with his horn. Three times he raised and bumped it to the ground. Then, seemingly, the tip of his horn, which must have become embedded in the woodwork, broke off and the whole weight of the lorry crashed down on his snout. Even his thick skin couldn't take such treatment, and, giving a roar of pain, he suddenly turned and crashed off through the bush.

I thought I deserved a few minutes' rest after such an adventurous encounter with five rhinos within half a mile and half an hour; but I didn't take them. I had already wasted far too much time and must now make with all speed to the scene of Rammal's siege. I checked that the improvised bomb was still intact in the compartment (rather remarkably, it was) and went on my way.

When I reached the escarpment I could see the little party encamped beside the defile. I parked the truck in the lee of a rock and began my upward climb. I had the bomb in my pocket and had to go very carefully for fear of damaging it. I was also considerably shaken up by my bumping in the truck; but in spite of this I wanted to get started on the attack on the fugitive.

I realized, of course, that the attack would have to be planned fairly carefully. Who would skirt the defile and throw the bomb? Would it be effective if it fell too far short of the cave? Was it a deep cave, and if so could Rammal get so far back from the entrance that it would be ineffective anyway? What was to be the procedure if Rammal was forced out of the cave by the gas? So far only the thrower of the bomb would be there. That man might himself be overcome by the gas. It was all very tricky and much of the plan must depend on improvisation. But common sense told me that Rammal was unlikely to be very far inside the cave, since he had to be his own lookout and presumably had a convenient point from which he could watch the defile without being easily seen himself.

I put all this to the policemen when I reached the encampment. They told me that there had been a guard on duty continuously at the defile and that, although the guard had periodically thrust his inquiring head round the corner, there had been neither sight nor sound of Rammal.

After considering a number of variations on the basic scheme to throw the bomb directly into the cave so that Rammal was forced into the open we decided that the simplest and most direct method was the best. All kinds of trickery were suggested, including deceptive approaches with white flags, calls to surrender, messages shot into the cave on arrows, and an armed attack on the cave under cover of darkness. I judged all of them to be too uncertain of success. An attack by darkness could have succeeded, but almost certainly someone would have been killed or injured, either by gunfire or by falling over the ledge that was the only way of approach. And in any case the D.C.'s instructions were to avoid any kind of bloodshed.

So there remained the simple throwing of the bomb. Not really so simple after all, for I had to round the defile (I decided that I'd do the throwing myself) and remain in full view for quite long enough for Rammal to pick me off before I could take aim and complete the throw. In any case, my aim might be bad or my range inadequate. I had only the haziest idea of the distance and would certainly have no time to measure up very accurately with my eye. The path on which I'd be forced to stand was barely wide enough for my two big feet, and the lobbing of the bomb might easily make me lose my balance and fall; and there was nothing at all to cling on to at that point, not even a root or branch projecting from the rock face.

However, it was a job to be attempted and I decided I'd lose no time. I thought it possible that Rammal might be asleep. He would almost certainly keep awake at night, prepared for an attack in the dark; so there was a chance that if I moved absolutely silently I might be able to negotiate the corner and manœuvre myself on to the open space before the cave without him being aware of my presence. On the other hand he might at this very moment be watching with wide open eyes. I should soon know.

My crêpe-soled chukka boots made absolutely no noise and I reached the defile without even alarming a buzzard I could see perched high on a ledge above me. The policemen were close behind me. They'd changed their service footwear for plimsolls and they too were quite silent. As for the natives with their naked feet—silence and sure-footedness were inherent with them. I had no fear that any of my companions would betray me by noise.

My instructions to them were to follow me round the defile only if I called or if there was a shot. I was unarmed myself, except for the bomb, so there could be no doubt about who was attacking whom. 'And for God's sake don't get too anxious on that ledge,' I whispered to the policeman immediately behind me now. 'Try to get round the corner too quickly and you'll fall base over apex downstairs.' I jerked my thumb downwards significantly and I heard the whispered message travel back along the file of men.

For a moment as I reached the ledge there was absolute quiet. Africa might have been an empty land. Then as I paused before stepping on to the ledge I listened and heard, faintly from the ground far below, the scuffling and faint reverberations as a small herd of zebras galloped across the plain.

Edging on to the ledge I paused and listened again for a full minute. But this time I was straining my ears to catch any sound from the cave.

There was nothing, nothing at all. I began to wonder if perhaps he'd escaped by some hidden passage through the hills. It was not outside the bounds of possibility. But no sense in wondering about that now.

'Here goes,' I murmured to myself. Inching forward round the rock face I suddenly realized that I was there, round the corner, that I must be in full view of my enemy. And as if to confirm it a burst of flame spurted at the cave entrance and the dust at my feet whirled up in a little eddy.

Accurate shooting, the devil! A revolver, too, so there'd be no reloading. I'd no time to consider aim or anything else now. I was round, on the open space, and I could see Rammal huddled at the entrance behind a rock, his pistol still smoking in his hand. He fired again, but this time I was prepared. I ducked, jumped to the left, and flung the little glass bottle—all in the same two seconds.

The bullet missed me by inches. I heard it *ping* on the rock face behind me. Next time he could hardly miss me.

I heard no sound of the bottle breaking; and for an instant I thought perhaps the glass had proved too tough. But it was all right. There was a puff of thick yellow smoke. It was some yards short of the entrance to the cave. Neither my aim nor my lobbing power was as good as I'd thought them to be. But—a miracle of good luck!—a factor we hadn't taken into consideration played its part now: a strong gusty wind suddenly billowed the pall of thick smoke towards the cave. And I heard Rammal's pistol fall to the ground as he put his hands up to ease the intolerable smarting of his eyes and came staggering out into the open.

DEATH OF A TERRORIST

THE poaching racket makes £50,000 a year for men like Rammal who run 'ivory rings': a serious consideration in the economics of a country like Kenya. And the effort to stamp out racketeering probably costs the administration as much again in money, besides absorbing the efforts and labour of police and investigators whose talents ought to be directed towards more profitable employment. But poaching of ivory fades into the insignificance of petty crime beside the long menace and ghastly achievements of Mau Mau.

The vicious and sadistic horrors of race hatred have no

place in this book; and in any case the story of Mau Mau has been written in the blood of its victims. Neither the eloquence to chronicle the crucifixion of those victims, nor the compassion I should christianly feel for the sins of the criminals, are mine to command. But I can tell, simply, what I know of the self-styled 'Field Marshal Sir Dedan Kimathi', the chief organizer and leader of the Mau Mau gang.

Kimathi was at one time a clerk on a dairy farm. I cannot say when or how he began to inject the sinister poison into the minds of his brothers of the Kikuyu. I know nothing at first hand of the power of his personality, only that that power was corruptly used to invoke race hatred of the wickedest kind—the kind that finds satisfaction for its lusts only in unspeakable torture. Race hatred is not by any means confined to coloured people: but I can find in my heart nothing but hatred for the individual, of whatever race, who inspires and invokes this base element of human nature.

Kimathi was just such a villain. With ruthless determination he organized the Kikuyu into gangs and worked out every detail of the hideous penalties that would be inflicted on those who refused to co-operate by swearing allegiance to the vile cause. The world knows of the Mau Mau oath and of the physical and mental tortures experienced by British residents and by Kikuyu workers who tried to escape the insidious corpuscles of evil in the bloodstream of their tribe. Their lives were lived out in fear and suspicion. The low whistle in the night, the summons to attend a sick child, the ordinary work of farm or plantation—no one could say at what time the figure would step from the shadow of the tree, the knife rip, or the shot ring out. Ritualistic violation of women and children became a commonplace, the severed head of a faithful servant might be found among the pig swill at feeding time, the grimly deflowered body of a British soldier or policeman might fall grotesquely from behind an outhouse door. Fear and sorrow killed each day, and nights were stained with the evil of the Mau Mau curse.

A state of emergency was declared by the government and in the now famous 'Operation Jack Scott' some of the group leaders were caught. But Kimathi had done his work well. Decentralization of the gangs underlined the futility of the security forces' efforts. One gang would be rounded up and half a dozen more would take its place. For a long time it seemed a hopeless task. The terrorists had every advantage on their side. It was easy to hide in the bush and mountains and forests; the 'screening' process instituted by the security forces, and having as its object the grading, into degrees of complicity, of all members of the Kikuyu tribe, was a clumsy and in many ways ineffective method of suppression; and, worst of all, Kimathi had a deputy, Stanley Mathenge, whose evil abilities were every bit as great as his own and who rekindled the flame of hate wherever it might be dying low. But after months of reigning terror it seemed that the patient weeding-out of all possible suspects was beginning to work. The security forces gained a new triumph by breaking up meetings of the infamous 'Mount Kenya Parliament'; in doing so, they learned that the tribal police of Kimathi's own district had rejected him and that they were willing to assist in his capture.

But the capture of Kimathi was another great task. Even with the help of ex-members of the Mau Mau it needed endless courage and perseverance to organize the highly complex system of trickery and ambush which was the only way of diminishing the numbers of those who hid away—in fear and trembling now not only of the penalties of Mau Mau but also of the growing design of law and order. Even under the decline of their reign of terror Kimathi and Mathenge held enough sway over their tribe to prevent any wholesale surrender of terrorists even when amnesties were offered by the government.

At last, however, the gangs dwindled to numbers that were no longer all-powerful; and then—this was in January 1956—the security forces were able to start work in earnest.

The death-knell of the terrorists was sounded on 23rd January, when two sub-leaders were captured in the Aberdare forest and persuaded to act as Special Branch spies. By maintaining contact with both Mau Mau and government forces they were able to get information which led to the ambushing of increasingly important gangsters. All the time the authorities were acquiring more and more knowledge of Kimathi and his immediate circle of henchmen; and in October of 1956 the Special Branch men had organized a system of spying, counter-spying and ambushing which would have done credit to M.I.5 and which brought in for trial Wambararia, Kimathi's brother, Kinyua Waweru, Ndungu Gicheru, and Theuri Makua—all leading organizers of the terror. Without these organizers many minor terrorists were helpless. They surrendered without further ado, and nearly all of them added to the quota of information that was piling up in the Kimathi file.

Kimathi himself had been tracked down several times to hideouts in the Aberdare forest; but he had so far always managed to escape. It was known that he had with him a woman member of the Mau Mau; and in the last week of October a half dozen security men working their way through the thick undergrowth heard a mad voice cry out:

'Stop! You are about to die! Field Marshal Sir Dedan Kimathi, leader of all men and of all armies, stands before you!'

Through the twitching foliage they glimpsed the figure

of Kimathi, clad in a leopard skin and rocking back and forth in glee. Beside him was his woman.

Regardless of danger, the little band of Kikuyu who had come to hate their megalomaniac leader thrust their way through the bush. They saw Kimathi and the woman flee across a clearing; but at the far edge the woman collapsed. She lay there on the ground panting with exhaustion but deep in her starved and weary eyes there glinted, unreasoning and powerful, a shard of hate. She made no attempt to rise or escape, and her captors could see that the indignity of being carried back to headquarters like a sack of potatoes was almost more than she could bear. They allowed her to suffer this indignity without comment.

Kimathi had escaped again; but now he was alone and hungry and he would be forced to seek help from his few remaining henchmen. Since it was known exactly where each one of these was to be found it was now only a matter of time before Kimathi was captured. Ambushes were set up at every point where he could leave the forest in search of food or help. Policemen, soldiers and Special Branch men waited. They waited by day and night, watching the movement of every shadow, listening for the sound of the footstep desperate for escape. They waited with their fingers on the triggers of their weapons, confident and grim, prepared to give no quarter to the creature who had set himself up as leader of a democratic body and had proved himself to be a dictatorial megalomaniac.

On the morning of the third Sunday in October they were rewarded. They heard the *chirr-chirr* warning note of a tick bird and watched it fly out from the forest. It was a little ahead of a tall figure in a leopard skin who, pressing himself almost invisibly against tree and bush, was attempting to gain the shelter of a ditch. With a good deal of luck he might have crawled along the ditch for some miles without being seen; he might even have escaped down one of the many streams feeding the Thika.

But this time he had no luck. He had been seen and he knew it was hopeless. With a last defiant gesture he ran. The finger of one of the members of his own tribe closed on the trigger and he fell with a harmless winging shot in the leg. The Kikuyu he had deluded and terrorized for so long closed in on him and their relentless hands closed about his arms and body. Kimathi's career had ended.

The trial was a long and impressive affair. But before it could even begin twenty translators and research workers had to get to work on the diaries and records Kimathi had kept. Like all megalomaniacs he had been unable to resist the temptation to put in permanent form the record of his crimes so that he could gloat over them even in retrospect. Elaborately written-up notebooks with carbon copies, complete lists of the personnel of the Mau Mau gangs, additional lists full of the names of people who had never been in Mau Mau but whose influential status had been traded on by Kimathi, diaries, plans of assassinations—everything needed to prove Kimathi's guilt was there. A friend of mine in the Special Branch of the Kenya Police told me that when they'd checked and collated and prepared the documentary evidence for submission to court there was a total of fourteen volumes.

Kimathi's trial by the Supreme Court began on 21st October. The Chief Justice, Sir Kenneth O'Connor, presided and the jurors were Kikuyu tribesmen. He was charged on three specific counts: illegal possession of firearms, illegal possession of ammunition, and the alleged murder of a forest guard in 1952. At the end of six days the assessors found him guilty of the unlawful possession of a revolver and the Chief Justice sentenced him to death. His subsequent appeal to the Court of Appeal was dismissed and the Judicial Committee of the Privy Council refused him leave to appeal to them. The man who'd so often been appealed to by the authorities was learning the effect of some of his own terrorist activities.

Kimathi was hanged in Nairobi prison on the morning of Monday, 18th February 1957. There was no magnificence in his life; and in his capture by the men of his own tribe there could have been for him only a degrading irony. The monstrous egocentricity of his activities long ago cloaked whatever may have been his original designs on behalf of his people. He did nothing but harm to the relationship between white and coloured races, and though the manner of his death may be morally unjustified in some men's eyes no one can feel anything but horror at the depth of his guilt, his complicity in the awful deaths of countless human beings.

MANHUNT XI

THE END

As I watched Rammal stagger out of the cave I yelled
out, 'Come on!' to my chaps. But there was no need:
they had heard the pistol shots and even as I ran forward
the first of the policemen followed me round the defile
and came running to my assistance. The Indian was
temporarily but completely blinded. He held both hands
before his face and was jerking his head up and down and
from side to side with the grotesque movements of a
disjointed doll. Tears were soaking through his fingers.
Even when he knew we were upon him he couldn't take
his hands away from his eyes. As we seized him he kicked
out with his foot. Then he began to struggle desperately
as we forced his hands down to put the handcuffs on.
Despair and pain had turned him into a flailing wind-
mill of sinew and bone. It was like trying to catch hold
of a steel spring under tension. Both the policemen and
I got kicks on the shin and elbows and in the face. I felt
my own right eye smarting from a blow from his shoulder
as he twisted and turned beneath our grasp. I'm no
lightweight, but power didn't seem to count for much
against such desperate agility.

We might, however, have forced Rammal's surrender
in a shorter time if the natives and the other policeman
had not by this time joined in the mêlée. There were
suddenly far too many of us and we all seemed to be
getting involved in an inextricable scrum in which our
own limbs rather than our captive's were being seized
and twisted. To the onlooker it must have appeared a
highly comic scene: nearly a dozen of us all mixed up in

a free-for-all with Rammal yelling blue murder somewhere at the bottom of the pile, clouds of dust being
scuffed up by our feet and enveloping us all, and the
whoops and choking grunts of the natives as they threw
themselves with wild enthusiasm but no design into the
scrum.

I was somewhere at the heart of things, clinging on to
the Indian and trying still to force him to the ground.
But everybody else was atop of us and it seemed to me
that we were all rolling far too close to the cliff edge to
be safe. And suddenly through the fork of someone's legs
I glimpsed the edge and an upside-down view of the
plain below. The contortions of the scuffle had imposed a
new danger on us all. A native foot was trampling on
my mouth, but by leaving go of whatever I'd been holding on to—I think it was Rammal's belt—I managed to
force it away and shout a genuinely desperate command.

They must have sensed the urgency in my voice, for,
as suddenly as the tangle of legs and arms had become
linked they were all miraculously unknotted and the
whole party of us had sprung away as if catapulted from
the cliff edge. Only Rammal lay now, momentarily
overpowered, with his head but a few inches from the
edge and one of his feet actually dangling over space.

In my leap from the edge I had fallen and banged my
head on a stone and I had to shake it hard to get rid of
the stars and double vision. We were all scrambling to
our feet—including, now, Rammal, who had handcuffs
dangling from one wrist and whose eyes were still streaming with tears. He covered his eyes with his hands again
and stood upright. My vision was just returning to
normal then, the mists and the stars were clearing. He
was swaying dangerously, his clothes were torn, and
although he now took his hands from his eyes and looked
about him dazedly I suddenly realized that with those
tears still pouring from his eyes he must be as blind as a

bat. And he was about to take a step towards the cliff edge.

'Look out!' I yelled at the top of my voice.

We all realized Rammal's predicament together and made a grab for him. It wasn't too late, but our farcical zealousness was almost the end of him—and of one of the policemen too—for we grabbed at Rammal a bit too enthusiastically and he was on his back again with his legs kicking in the air and the policeman pinning them down and tripping and falling perilously near the edge as he did so.

But with further scuffling we managed to pull Rammal and the policeman to safety. Then I yelled at them all to stand back and I clipped the handcuffs on to Rammal's other wrist. Then I got the two policemen to hold on to him. He was winded now and still in pain from his smarting eyes: but the effect of the gas was beginning to wear off. I could see that he was looking at us through the diminishing tears with an expression of extreme contempt. And I had to admit that all in all it had been a pretty poor show. There were nine of us and he'd given us all a fight. I had no one but myself to blame for that. The natives had naturally taken my summons for assistance literally; no one could blame them for their misdirected enthusiasm. 'Come on,' I said to Rammal; and I didn't regret the grudging enthusiasm in my voice. 'Show's over now.'

'I made you plenty of trouble,' he said with a smirk I instantly resented.

'And plenty for yourself,' I said coldly, 'as you'll see when we get back.'

I wasn't taking any more risks or having any more nonsense. I sent one of the policemen ahead round the defile with Rammal immediately behind him, followed by the other policeman. I told them to wait for us round the corner and not to let go of him even though he was handcuffed. I'd seen too much of his ingenuity and determination.

We followed round in procession. Then we rested for a while in the encampment, getting our breath back and repairing such damage to our clothing as we could manage. The natives scored heavily there, since they had no clothing to speak of; but the policemen's uniforms were dirty, crumpled and torn and I was glad that without any suggestion from me they exhibited enough pride in them to go off and wash them in a nearby stream and press them with flat sun-heated stones before we began the homeward journey.

When all this had been done and we'd fed and rested we started in procession down the slope of the escarpment to the waiting truck. Rammal was resigned now: with true oriental philosophy he had accepted the inevitable. He had been overpowered but he was aware of his personal triumph and he wasn't going to let any of us forget it. I got one of the policemen to drive while I sat in the back with the rest of the party and forced myself to stare out Rammal's contemptuous smiling insolence with all the indifference I could contrive. But I admit that it had to be contrived. To tell the truth, I was feeling pretty needled that he'd so nearly got the better of us. At the back of my resentment, no doubt, was the knowledge that I'd wasted a lot of time on him that could certainly have been devoted more pleasurably, if not more profitably, to ranging for game. No use crying over spilt milk, though. And anyway, I told myself, it's an adventure that's sharpened our wits a bit.

We delivered Rammal to the D.C.'s office. He cast a covert glance at our dishevelled clothes and a faint smile lit his eyes. The natives were dismissed and the D.C. formally arraigned Rammal and he was taken to a cell to await his appearance before the magistrates the following morning. I couldn't help reflecting that it all seemed very flat and dull after the dance he'd led us. The D.C. must have read my thoughts, for he said:

'It's always the same when it's all over. You'd best get back at the butt end of a rifle again as soon as possible. Eh?'

'Well,' I said, 'I can't say I'll be sorry to turn my thoughts back to game again. This last week's been a bit confusing, and the ways I've been fooled by that little monkey you've just put in the jug are just nobody's business.'

Noel Hardy came from an inner office to thank me. 'It may have seemed a pretty poor hunt to you, J.A., but it means a hell of a lot to us—and to African economics and industry as a whole. I don't have to tell you that. And anyway you had what excitement there was. My party did nothing but a grand tour of the Yatta Plateau.'

The D.C. said:

'I think the way to look at it is this: if the trial goes well and we get a conviction and sentence for Rammal the bottom will be out of the racket. Other gangs and subsidiaries will be weakened and will collapse. Poaching won't be worth the risk. We'll have too many men eavesdropping on the eavesdroppers in those back-street coffee shops in Mombasa. And if the means of disposal dries up there'll be no sense in continuing poaching. I don't think you or many other people realized that if poaching had continued at the rate it was going on the elephant race could have died out in Kenya in a couple of years. Did you?'

'I'd had a shrewd suspicion.' I got up to go. 'Well, I hope you get your conviction all right.'

'Thanks to you, J.A., I guess we will.'

I went off up to the hospital next, to thank Claude for inventing the bomb that had been so useful. He smiled and bowed. 'Delighted to be of assistance. A simple thing, and the simple things are the things that work—always.'

While we chatted he told me an interesting thing about arrow poison; and although I'd just been caused a lot of trouble by natives who used it one way—'You know the proverb, sir, about the bad wind that blows not anybody any good?'—it seemed that a lot of research had been going on in another direction.

Over the whole of the east side of the African continent, from Eritrea in the north, down through Kenya, Mozambique, Rhodesia, and Transvaal, and as far towards the middle of Kenya as Lake Rudolph, you can find the inconspicuous but quite pretty tree which is the source of the arrow poison used by the natives. The *Acokanthera* belongs to the botanical group *Apocynacea* and has dark green stiff leaves not unlike those of the laurel—though not so shiny—and small lilac-scented flowers which bloom at the same time as the grape-sized purple fruit. The brewing of the poison, which is carried out with much ceremony, music and dancing, is basically a boiling of the leaves, fruit and bark of the *Acokanthera* and other vegetable and animal oddments in a big pot for some eight or nine hours, during which time the brew becomes a thick black paste which is smeared round the shafts of arrows just behind the head and wrapped around with thin bark to keep it soft while the arrows are in store. But the actual formulae and methods of distillation vary from tribe to tribe and are handed down as tribal secrets from generation to generation by the elders of the Giriama, the Ndorobo, the Wasanya, the Wakamba, and the Wanduruma people.

Claude told me how, many years ago, Peter Bally, a botanist at the Coryndon Museum, had begun to study the *Acokanthera* not only as a botanical subject but also ethnologically, as a characteristic poison of the East African tribes. His researches led him to make contact with Professor Reichstein of Basle University, who was awarded the Nobel prize in 1950 and who was intensely interested in the biochemical values of poisons. Claude himself was asked to help in collecing specimens and information.

'The Professor and Mr. Bally were interested in a project which I, a medical man, was also most concerned to assist. They believed there might be valuable properties in the *Ouabaine*—that is, in Somali, the poison—which might, if separated and analysed, make a drug of good effect.' He undid his white coat and pointed to his chest. 'For the heart. Rather like Digitaline but perhaps even more powerful when a weakened heart has to be renewed in power.

'They told me they needed to know the ingredients of the brew the Giriama people concoct and asked me if I could assist to find out.' He smiled with gentle humour. 'It is so often believed—and, of course, especially by unworldly and charming men such as professors and botanists—that one negro has only to go to another and ask him the inmost secrets of tribal lore and he will be told. I need perhaps not have to tell you, Mr. Hunter, that this is not at all the case. Such secrets are guarded with Masonic care. And it would in any case be completely unhonoured for me, with my Arts Bachelor degree and my Medical Doctorate, to gain knowledge in this dubious way.' He paused and smiled again; then: 'Except for reasons in accordance with the Hippocratic law, which is, as you know, to do all one can for the total good of mankind. So my conscience was easy on this target when I went to see one of the Giriama people and made a friend of him. He was the doctor of the tribe and I appealed to him as one medical man to another. There is no need to go into the detail. In the end he was kind enough to give me the formula, and the detail of location of the other plants we needed to know. Because, you see, it was the extra elements that would be the necessary ones.

'There is a plant which is called in Latin *Sapium Madagascarensis*, a quite rare plant, which when touched on the skin makes inflammation so that the poison from the *Acokanthera* gets into the blood quicker. And another, the *Dioscorea*, which is an insignificant little flower with a bulb like the shape of a human liver and a hairy root-growth which is as extremely poisonous as the *Acokanthera* but with a different effect. Besides these three, the Giriama use another element in their concoction, and this is for what we should call the psychological effect.

'You know the Elephant Shrew? This little animal with the long nose always runs in a straight line when it is being chased. So the Giriama say that if the body of an Elephant Shrew is allowed to decay a little after death and is then thrown into the pot with the mixture of plants it will cause any animal killed by arrow poison to run straight instead of tumbling off sideways into the bush.

'All this was of great interest to Mr. Bally and Professor Reichstein, and I was able to send them specimens of the plants, also some seedlings of a special development of *Acokanthera* grown only by the Giriama. Mr. Bally tells me that they are now well on the road of discovery and that they presently hope to publish a treatise in which will be explained methods of distilling a new drug that may be of supreme value in cases of heart diseases. So it is true, Mr. Hunter, that there is progress continually from even the most evil things.'

Yes, it was true, I reflected. Most platitudes are. And, like most platitudes which can be related to one's recent efforts, it gave me a warm glow. Quite unjustifiably, it half seemed as if the manhunt that had robbed me of quite a bit of my proper work had had an outcome that would benefit mankind in a much larger way than merely by the putting down of a gang of ivory poachers in East Africa. With a few more encouraging words from Claude

I think I could have believed that it was I personally who had achieved something in the world of scientific medicine. It was a pleasantly puffed-up feeling and I started off home very satisfied with myself and my life in general.

Hilda as always was there to welcome me. She knew at once that this task of manhunting had given me very little satisfaction in spite of the false cheer I had fluffed up my feathers with. Praise be, she is not one of those demanding women who need to know immediately you return every detail of what has happened since last she saw you. She simply saw now that I was tired; she poured me a drink and took one for herself and waited till I was sat down and relaxed a bit. Then she told me the one bit of news she knew would cheer me.

'John, another consignment of materials was delivered to the house today; and there was a note from the shipping company: the furniture's on its way from home.'

I nodded, pleased. But I reminded her, '*This* is home—this and *Hunter's Lodge* when a few more bricks have been delivered and stuck together.'

It was her turn to be pleased. It was she who long ago had recognized that Africa was in all but my birth my native land, and, devoting herself to my happiness rather than her own, had set at nothing any longing she may have had to return to Ventnor, Isle of Wight. It perhaps can be a very terrible thing for a woman to face a lifetime in a strange country; to be married to a man whose pursuits she can share but not enjoy; to be the centre of a home that has no social life, and where danger is always in the air. To remain calm and devoted and busy, to raise six children and watch them, and then one day to find them all grown and gone and to be alone typing their father's reminiscences just to find the same endless talk of *safaris*. . . . Well, there it is; but perhaps it is warming to know—as she must—that she is really the heart of things, the mainspring—mine and the family's.

We have four sons and two daughters, and when I think back to 1919 when the eldest, Doreen, was born I can recall only three of those confinements when I was within call. In 1927, when David was born, I was hunting a rogue elephant with Sidney Waller, another big-game chap—whose wife also was expecting a baby; in 1923 I was out on a *safari* from which I didn't return till Sheila was nearly a week old; and in 1925 I came back from a grand elephant shoot to learn that Dennis had arrived. But I've not heard any reproaches about this. All these children have grown up and become architects and managers of coffee plantations and wives of army colonels and ferry superintendents and wanderers, and they've all gone away as children should— some of them only to Nairobi, though!—and now Hilda has more time to read and type my books and deal with the 'Come immediately and shoot three lions' messages; but no more time to be devoted, for she has always found all the time in the world for that.

GRAND SAFARI

I RETURNED from that manhunt quite unsensationally, just as I have set down, with no more—and no more deserved—than a nod of thanks from the D.C. and a pleasantly self-satisfied ride back in a fifteen-hundred-weight truck from Makindu hospital. It was just a job. Hardy and I had set out in the International a couple of weeks before and now we had pulled in our quarry. There wasn't anything to go down in the Rowland Ward record book; it was just, as Claude had pointed out, a part of the Austin Reed service. And like many another hunt it had left me weary—but without the tangible and worthwhile evidence of the pair of tusks to be held up and photographed or the gift of a goat from a native farmer whose crops had been saved from the depredations of elephant or rhino. It wasn't disappointing exactly, it was just that the hunting of beasts holds for me all the excitement which my years in Africa have conditioned me to and the hunting of a man, however cunning and elusive, seemed a poor substitute; though Rammal certainly offered excitements of another kind. But I think a note of slight dissatisfaction is altogether the wrong note on which to end a book. I have a feeling that a paean of extravagance would not be out of place, for a bit of splendour occasionally comes into the undecorative life of the hunter, and certainly nothing of an extravagant nature has so far entered this book; in fact, such excitements as it has had to offer have been excessively plain and simple and the undertones of a spartan sort of existence have been murmuring along in the background most of the way.

Let me tell, then, of one of the many *safaris* I have conducted for Indian Maharajahs. These fabulously wealthy men have always been encouraged to come to the game fields of Kenya because of their lavish spending power; but quite apart from this all those I have known as clients have been completely charming men, invariably educated at the major public schools and universities of England, and with highly developed sporting instincts. Their own country, of course, offers splendid facilities for big game hunting—especially for the tiger, an exclusively Asian animal—but nonetheless those princes with a special fondness for the *safari* always seek sport in Africa sooner or later.

Naturally, with their practically unlimited wealth

they are able to indulge whatever fancies they may have.
Weapons of the finest quality, unlimited bearers and
transport, reconnaissance aircraft, elaborate food—
everything is theirs to command. But where these advantages might be within the grasp of any rich man, the
princes of India, however elaborate their arrangements,
are nearly always excellent shots and have genuinely,
and highly developed, sporting characters; while the
casual European or American millionaire is likely to be
throwing his money around merely to be able to say he's
been on *safari*.

The Maharajah I most clearly remember was ruler of
one of the southern Indian states. Quite a young man,
he was inclined to corpulence and had become a little
worried about it and had sought advice from his doctors
and soothsayers. They, recognizing that what His Highness needed more than anything was some exercise, but
no doubt feeling that they could hardly tell him this as a
blunt statement, prescribed for him a tiger hunt and
assured him that by the time he had shot his hundredth
tiger their prayers and spells would have worked and he
would be restored to normal weight. But they had not
taken into account his princely idea of a tiger hunt.
This was to make elaborate arrangements and go off on
safari through the Indian jungle in an armoured car,
from which he quickly shot a hundred tigers without any
effect at all on his weight—not surprisingly. Puzzled and
disappointed, he visited his advisers again and presumably told them he didn't think much of their advice
or their spells. No doubt they were terrified and expected
to be beheaded immediately; but when this didn't happen they slowly began to realize that His Highness's
western education had gone a long way towards cancelling
out such merciless notions. So they summoned up their
courage and told His Highness more or less directly that
what they'd meant was that he should shoot tigers by

hunting them as a pedestrian, and that unless he made himself sweat a bit he'd get fatter than ever. He saw the wisdom of this at once. But at the same time he realized that his princely station didn't really allow him to go careering through the jungle villages, in full view of countless subjects whose religious devotion to him was the heritage of untold generations, on his own two feet. This wasn't the reasoning of a conceited tyrant but of a ruler deeply versed in understanding of his people and full of consideration for the religion he represented. He thought about the matter for a couple of days and decided that he'd go on *safari* in another country altogether, then there'd be no embarrassment to anyone. He chose Africa. And that was how I came to be engaged as a guide and adviser on what must have been one of the most spectacular *safaris* ever to glamorize the bushland of Kenya and Tanganyika.

His Highness's ambassadors—no less impressive a word will do to describe these gentlemen—arrived ahead of him and interviewed me in their hotel in Nairobi. They were grave, charming, considerate and beautifully dressed. But they left no doubt in my mind at all of the lavish scale on which the *safari* was to be conducted. No detail had been overlooked and no expense was to be spared. They had arranged for the transportation of everything and everyone to Nairobi and when all had been safely gathered in and His Highness had arrived the administration was to be left entirely to me. His Highness expected good sport and was out to capture several records. The ambassadors hoped—and, I inferred, expected—that everything would go like clockwork. I told them I accepted the commission gladly. I had conducted Maharajahs before and I knew that however elaborate their fancies one at least knew how one stood with them. And I had a feeling that in this case the Maharajah and I would get on famously.

A few days later the equipment began to arrive. If I hadn't had full details in advance from the ambassadors I should have begun to wonder if I was dealing with the effects of some gigantic film company embarking on the making of a big-game film to end all big-game films. Vehicles (including an armoured car!) had been shipped from England and America and included a mobile wireless receiving and transmitting station, a van for cinematography which included a screen and projector and armchair seats from which the Maharajah could watch wild animal films, an elaborately equipped kitchen, generating plants, lorries to carry emergency storage batteries, a medical van with an X-ray unit, mobile offices, canteens and water tanks, and a royal caravan in which was a miniature but beautifully furnished bedroom and a drawing-room holding a small piano and an electrical reproducer—the caravan hauled on an articulated trailer powered by a Scammell engine. In addition to this extensive fleet of vehicles, which I was relieved to know would form a base camp only and would perforce keep to the main roads, there were numerous small trucks and motor cycles and a fine assortment of marquees and tents to be carried by native bearers. There were also a number of Elsan chemical lavatories and gaily striped canvas booths to put them in.

The disposal of this vast army of *safari* furniture was quite simple; open space is not lacking in Kenya; and since it didn't all arrive together, but came up from Mombasa on a series of specially chartered railway wagons, I was able to organize the establishment of our first base camp at leisure.

Naturally my first thoughts were for His Highness's guns. These had been shipped out in a series of ant-proof and moisture-proof boxes which were works of art in themselves. They were as magnificent a collection of rifles and smooth-bores as ever I've seen—all of them

built to measure by Holland and Holland and James
Purdey. Their balance and finish would have made the
eyes of any connoisseur brighten with pleasure. The work
of these great gunmakers is always supreme, and even a
Maharajah can't get better guns than the best; but His
Highness had been able to express his individuality in
small ways. For example, the walnut stocks had been
specially selected for the beauty of their grain and had
velvet covers to prevent scratching. I spent a long time
examining and delighting in these weapons—a whole
magnificent armoury of them.

His Highness had arranged for licences to shoot a liberal
quota of game animals and also had special permits to
cover elephants and rhinos. He even had permits to kill
giraffes—innocent and completely stupid animals which
I sincerely hoped he would leave alone, since they are
quite harmless and decorative in a lunatic way. He
wanted particularly lion, buffalo, roan antelope and
Thomson's gazelle—and as many world records as could
be managed. I had planned an itinerary for him which
covered much of Masailand and a vast stretch of the
Serengeti plain as far west as Simiyu, which is very fine
lion country. It would take us many weeks to hunt the
country properly and I hoped there'd be plenty of opportunity to get the Maharajah trapesing through the bush
on his two feet and sweating some of his royal fat off.
Incidentally, the ambassadors presented me with a copy
of Rowland Ward's book of game records. Rich clients
invariably do this so that there shall be no doubt of the
size beasts they expect me to produce, and through the
years I have come to hate the sight of it. But there are
quite a number of my clients' names in it, and, as I
flipped through the pages I noticed the name of Major
R. V. Bruce, who was a client of mine in 1923 and shot
the record Thomson's gazelle which had a horn length
of 16¾ inches. It has remained a world's record ever

since and I wondered if we'd ever find a 'Tommy' to beat it and thus get the Maharajah's name into the antelope pages of the book. Well, that remained to be seen.

The Maharajah himself arrived at Nairobi airport in his private air liner about a week after the last of the *safari* equipment had been delivered. The ambassadors and the rest of the retinue went to meet him and escort him to the palatial caravan, which he was to make his headquarters till we were ready to start. He was a charming and intelligent man wearing well-cut khaki drill and a turban with a jewel in it. I never saw him without the turban during the whole *safari*, yet somehow he contrived not to appear overdressed or even particularly conspicuous. I warmed to him at once when he said as soon as I'd been presented, 'We'll have a splendid time, Hunter; a splendid time. I feel it in my bones.' I saw the gleam of sportsmanship in his eye, and as he looked out over the terrain he added, 'Already I've seen more game animals wandering about than I see in a month in India. We must start as soon as possible.'

In fact we started the next morning. Natives popped up from everywhere to see the extraordinary convoy move off. The jungle drums had been working overtime and whole villages made processions to watch us start and tag along beside the road. From the Maharajah's caravan came the high-powered but extraordinarily inept music of Rachmaninoff's C-minor piano concerto played through the electric amplifier. Buffalo and antelope continued to graze, quite indifferent to what must have been quite a new noise to them, and the natives who carried blowing and banging instruments of their own blew and banged on them every now and again with a complete disregard for Rachmaninoff's opposition.

I learnt during that *safari* that the Maharajah was very devoted to music. At home he maintained a private

orchestra to accompany him in his own playings of all
the great concertos. I heard him play on the little piano
in the caravan and I must say his technique was far
above the average, though not always adequate to cope
with the Chopin and Liszt pieces he attempted. Sometimes he was brought to a standstill by the mountainous
difficulties of the B-minor Scherzo or *Campanella*; then he
would scramble all the notes together, throw up his hands
and cry, 'Bothersome, very! Not nearly so simple as
hunting.'

For some days we zig-zagged across Masailand bag-
ging a lion here and an elephant there. The main convoy
had been parked now that we were in dense country and
we were travelling 'light'. This meant that we had the
armoured car for His Highness and me to travel in, a
couple of trucks with storage batteries and other equipment, a crowd of natives who doubled the duties of
scouts, porters and gun bearers, and a constant shuttle
service of armed motor cyclists between us and the base
camp bringing up food in vacuum containers. I never
really understood why His Highness bothered to bring
such elaborate kitchen equipment with him, for his meals
invariably consisted of rice prepared in different ways
or goat's flesh—and female goat at that. However, mine
not to reason why. I foraged for my own and the bearers'
food, knowing that they'd be kept far happier with a
constant supply of fresh antelope meat than with the
highly seasoned food from the Maharajah's ritzy
kitchen.

His Highness proved himself a fine sport. Although he
had all those permits and could have gone round popping
off guns here, there and everywhere I was delighted to
find that he held my own views about the indiscriminate
killing of game animals. There was one instance too,
when he deliberately allowed an animal to get the better
of him because he admired her dauntless challenge.

This was down on the Serengeti plain and it was the day we'd decided to try for a record Thomson's gazelle. The plain was a wonderful place for antelope of all kinds —the whole range of species from dik-dik to eland grazed and gambolled there in thousands. There were so many of them that they seemed to find security in their own numbers and barely edged away as we crept over the bushland in the armoured car with our heads and shoulders sticking out of the twin turrets. I must say I'd become heartily sick of the task of peering through my binoculars at the endless groups of antelope day after day searching for a record 'Tommy', and my eyes felt tired. But there came the moment when a herd of several hundred galloped past us and I chanced to spot a fine buck sporting a good pair of horns which looked as if they might be of record length and were also evenly matched and shapely. The herd pulled up half a mile or so away and we pursued them in the armoured car. Behind us came the small truck carrying the Maharajah's doctor and secretary. We all dismounted fifty or so yards away and then moved up on the herd stealthily but without going to any great trouble to conceal ourselves. The gazelles continued to graze and I had some difficulty in picking out the big fellow again; but suddenly I saw him and nudged the Maharajah. The range was easy and he shot the beast cleanly. It fell, and the rest of the herd, alarmed, began to panic. But none of them galloped far away. They eyed us curiously, not quite sure what had happened in their midst, and we moved up with bearers and truck to measure the gazelle and load it. The horns were 17 inches.

'Whatever else I fail to get, I shall get my name in Ward for this one,' the Maharajah said. But he spoke too soon.

At that moment the Indian secretary began gesticulating to draw our attention to another 'Tommy' that stood

a hundred yards or so off to the right. 'The biggest ever!'
he said. 'That one!'

I wasn't at all sure personally, but the Maharajah
seemed to agree and it was his *safari* anyway, so off we
went in the armoured car to pursue our new quarry. He
had taken fright by now and was galloping away across
the plain. The rest of the herd followed, they were by
now thoroughly disturbed and were finding cover. It was
plain that we should never catch our 'biggest ever' beast.
There is no sport in hounding terrified animals to death—
the Maharajah saw eye to eye with me over that. He
smiled blandly and told the driver to turn. 'We'll return
and pick up the other.'

As we drove back I saw vultures hovering over the spot
where we'd left the gazelle, but to our utter astonishment
the body had gone. I could scarcely believe my eyes. It
was like the disappearance of the body in a whodunit.

'Now where the hell——'

The Maharajah pointed to the left. A hundred yards
away through the bush there was a big lioness carrying
our gazelle as a labrador would a pheasant. His Highness
was laughing, and I couldn't help tipping a smile myself
at the audacious way she'd carried it off from under our
very noses.

Quickly we followed in the car. I'd never seen anything like this happen before and I fully expected the
lioness to drop her capture and bolt as soon as she saw us
coming. But not she! She'd got it and she evidently
intended to keep it. There were probably some cubs
awaiting her in her lair.

She'd made thick cover by now. We could take the
car no further. But the Maharajah had the glint of enthusiasm in his eyes and he signalled me to alight with
him and follow her. We pushed through the thorn for a
quarter-mile or so and still she went on ahead, showing
no sign of tiring or of dropping the gazelle. Then we

seemed to close up on her. We got to within about twenty
yards of her and she suddenly dropped the body and
turned, snarling, to make a feint towards us. I am sure
she would have charged, and I nudged the Maharajah
to take aim, at the same time raising my own Holland
to cover him in case he should miss. But he shook his head
and retreated a few paces, pulling me back with him.
Immediately the lioness cancelled her threat to charge
us, picked up the gazelle again and turned to make off—
but not without a pause and a backward glance to make
sure we'd given up any idea of following her.

'She's dauntless and determined,' His Highness said.
'Let her keep it. We'll find another just as good.'

In point of fact we never did. The nearest we got was a
16-incher, and the illustrious name never went in the
illustrious book after all. But I don't think the Maraja-
jah minded. He'd begun to enjoy himself so much (and
had already lost some pounds in weight) that he didn't
seem to bother about records any more. Which made
better sport for everyone.

At the end of each day a motor-cyclist despatch rider
was sent back to the base convoy bearing full details of
the bag. This news was then put over the air by the
mobile transmitter, picked up in Nairobi and put out
again from there on the permanent short-wave apparatus
for transmission to India. It would then appear as a news
item in the papers of the Maharajah's state the following
day. 'His Highness today shot a buffalo, a kudu and a
fine black-maned lion.'

This was usually the last job before we made camp for
the night. It was left entirely to me to decide whether it
was worthwhile returning to the base convoy—which of
course could keep up with us only so far as roads would
allow—or whether we should pitch our tents at the most
suitable spot nearby. His Highness liked to be able to
get back to his caravan and play his piano; and the ease

with which he used to switch from the aesthetics of hunting to the aesthetics of music never ceased to amaze me: he would hand his rifle to his bearer or secretary after his final shot of the day and murmur, 'I shall approach the *Polichinelle* tonight;' and this even after a quite gruelling day in which we might have travelled some hundreds of square miles in the armoured truck and done a good trek through bushland tangled with wait-a-bit thorn. But on the other hand he liked to be on the scene of the next day's manœuvres if possible, so that no time should be wasted in getting to the new venue. Whatever I decided he accepted without question, and I must say that in this respect alone he was the ideal client. So many people hire you for the benefit of your advice and experience and ignore both at the first opportunity. If, then, I decided to pitch camp in some convenient spot near the scene of our last bag he would invite me to dine with him in his tent and afterwards encourage me to tell him of experiences of mine which might parallel his during that particular day. For instance, on the day the lioness stole the 'Tommy' from him he was most anxious to know if I could recollect any similar instance of beast challenging man for possession of prey.

'Not in my own experience,' I told him; 'but I recall Gordon Harvey, a chum of mine, telling me of something similar—and, in a way, more remarkable.'

In that case, Gordon was hunting in Masailand and spotted a pair of gazelles feeding on a fringe of grassland. Their appearance was opportune, for his porters had had no food and had become a little unco-operative and he was anxious to get something rather special to placate their feelings of resentment. He had no difficulty in downing one of the gazelles with a single bullet and was on his way to claim the body when he realized that a remarkable thing had happened: his single shot had killed two gazelles. They must have been feeding side by side and the bullet had passed straight through the head of one into the other.

Approaching the bodies with high glee he suddenly saw two lionesses appear on the scene. They had evidently been stalking the two gazelles which Gordon had conveniently shot for them. They now picked up a carcass each and began to move off. Gordon bawled at the top of his voice and the larger lioness momentarily dropped her burden and turned to face him, snarling in a most malicious way. He was but a few yards off by this time and saw that she was in earnest and about to charge. He fired without further ado and without having time to take proper aim; but the bullet went home. In the very act of tautening her limbs for the charge the lioness turned two complete somersaults as she was hit. But after landing she recovered immediately and prepared to charge again—the bullet apparently only having penetrated her flank. This time Gordon dropped to one knee and took careful aim. But in mid-air the lioness lurched and fell again to the ground—without the trigger being squeezed a second time. The first shot had evidently been effective but had had a delayed action. Meanwhile the other lioness had made off with the second gazelle, but at least Gordon was able to claim the first— as well as receiving an object lesson in caution.

As it happened, it was only a few days later when the Maharajah himself was to experience a quite remarkable case of a beast recovering after apparent death.

We had been moving southward down the Serengeti plain and every day we had had many successes and much pleasure. His Highness, beautifully turned out in fresh khaki drill each morning by his valet, had become more and more attached to the thrills of hunting on foot. He had not scorned even the royally undignified methods of the old-style tracker. 'Sometimes I seem to be crawling for miles on my belly through this cursèd thornland,' he said; but it was plain that he was really enjoying every minute of it. I pointed out to him everything that seemed interesting and if it was something that specially appealed to him he would signal to his secretary to make a note. Hints on identifying depredatory elephants by the grains of maize in their droppings, observations on the way stream banks had been widened and broken down by beasts seeking salt, the ways of some animals who live on the moisture to be found in grasses, and of the cunning of others in finding water secreted in hollow caves and boles—these were perennially interesting to him. 'You see, I have only made the kills before, Hunter. Nothing has been explained to me. It is so fascinating.' He was shiveringly impressed when I told him that a single blow of a lion's forearm is in fact capable of felling an ox; and as it happened we several times came on the remains of hyenas, mere grisly squashings of mush because they had gone too close to some lion's kill and had been flattened in revenge by a rippling forepaw striking them blows with the equivalent of half a ton behind them. Each night the secretary's notes would be sent back to base with the radiogram dealing with the day's activities, and each morning they would come back typed on gold-edged paper and bound into a red leather book which the Maharajah would keep in the armoured car along with the specially bound copy of the estimable Rowland Ward. Not, he explained, for publication but for a record of a happy time.

We reached a village one day where there was considerable unrest. Natives clustered in groups round their mud huts and clearly were very depressed about something. His Highness asked me to go and find out if it was our presence that disturbed them. But the native chief explained to me that far from being antagonistic towards us they were thinking of approaching the big *bwana* to ask if he could help them. They were suffering from the effects of marauding elephants on their crops and had been unable to deal with them. The crops were ripening and they would be ruined if something wasn't done quickly.

I put it to the Maharajah. We had already shot several fine tuskers and he was quite satisfied with his score; but he agreed that it would be a good thing if this time he could really be of use and told me to tell the chief that we'd make it our business to track the marauders down and scare them off.

Off we started next day. There was no difficulty in finding the first indications: the great beasts had milled all over the fields of ripening maize, trampling and up-rooting as they went and leaving dollops of dung all over the place. All that day we moved on, abandoning the transport whenever we came to dense cover; looking for signs of the elephants' passing among the tangle of thorn and brush, and picking up the trail again when it emerged into the open. It was nearing mid-afternoon of the following day when we found droppings that were warm and steaming. And shortly after that His Highness nudged me: three large brown bulls were visible through the foliage—all backside-on to us, not by any means the best position. 'You drive them out, I'll cover them as they emerge,' the Maharajah said. But I pointed out that I was responsible for his safety. The risks were really too grave. He signed assent and kept by my side.

Hurriedly I skirted the thicket and took a right and left from my D/B at the two flanking beasts of the trio. Both dropped immediately and there was a tremendous cracking of wood and foliage as they fell. Desperately I tried to reload so that I could get the third beast; but this one was His Highness's: he'd got his rifle up and had fired—an orthodox ear shot—before I had the dead shells out of the breech.

So there we were with our three culprits all down with-

in the space of half a minute: one of those lucky occasions
—another time one might track a trio for days and
manage to kill only one or two.

The Maharajah strode over to his elephant and sat
astride its neck. His pleasure was like a schoolboy's—and
well merited, for he'd timed and aimed his shot splendidly.
I joined him at the other end of the body. It was a hot
day, the going had been fairly tough for the last half-mile
or so, and there was a certain simple satisfaction in doing
the big-game hunter act and putting one's foot proudly
on the carcass—the 'alone-I-did-it' feeling. His Highness
beamed and swung his legs in their now rather less than
immaculate trousers against the elephant's neck. I
reached up and pulled an unripe coconut and split it
and handed half to His Highness. We drank to our day's
work. One of the native boys now came through the
bush and cut the elephants' tails off—this they do
because the hairs are supposed to be lucky and are made
into bangles. The bearers were very high spirited—a
successful shoot invariably inspires them to joyful antics
—and they were dancing and jostling round the three
mountainous bodies. When they cut off the tail of the
elephant we were sitting on I remember thinking I felt a
slight twitching of the body; but it seemed nothing to
take any notice of. If I'd considered it at all I should have
come to the conclusion that it was a reaction of the
nervous system. Anyway, time was getting on then and we
decided we'd return to the village that night and tell the
villagers the glad news before pitching camp for the
night. Bearers and everyone else were loaded into the
armoured car and the small trucks and we drove off.
There was great rejoicing in the village that night. The
Maharajah was made quite a hero and presented with
an elephant's hair ring made from the tail of the beast he
had shot.

Next day we wanted to continue our *safari* along its

originally planned route, so we sent natives up to cut the
tusks from the elephants we'd shot. They returned with
two pairs of tusks and the news that His Highness's
elephant had got up and walked away after death,
leaving his tail behind him! According to them it was the
devil's work; but my own view was that the Maharajah's
bullet had just missed the brain housing and caused
temporary shock instead of death. I was horrified when
I realized how lacking in caution I had been—and with
the object lesson of Gordon Harvey's lion fresh in my
mind, too. But the knowledge that an injured elephant
was wandering abroad was even more lamentable. Alas,
there was nothing we could do, for he would be miles
away by now.

The natives who had gone up to cut the tusks out were
highly delighted because they had found particles of
stick and thorn in the skulls. These scraps, which work
their way into the tough hide as a result of continual
passage through thick undergrowth, are much prized as
charms and cure-alls. The tusks themselves were magnificent—one pair 260 pounds and the other 230 pounds.
His Highness had himself photographed in the usual
way with the tusks framing him in an arch; and the
renewed festivities by the villagers in our honour with
dancing and a deal of palm wine drinking were also
filmed. There were some heavy showers of rain during
the night and by morning thousands of wild flowers were
freshly blooming—the whole of the area surrounding the
village glowed as if with a multitude of pink and crimson
stars.

One of the Maharajah's many charms was his inexhaustible curiosity. Although he always seemed satisfied
with the answers I gave him to his many questions, he
preferred to have practical demonstrations if possible—
'One sees for oneself.' So when he asked me what food lions
prefer if they have the choice I suggested an experiment.

'We'll bait one and you shall see for yourself,' I said.

Next day we fortunately found ourselves in an area where the variety of game was immense. Wildebeest, hartebeest, ostrich, rhino, hippo, elephant, zebra—seldom have I seen such a richly populated square mile or two; and there were game birds in endless variety—muscovy duck, several kinds of francolin, guinea fowl and grouse. In every direction herds and groups of creatures could be seen. It was like being in the wholesale department of an animal store.

We approached this spot along a track which was just about wide enough to take the main convoy. The Maharajah was in his caravan writing some letters and above him the royal flag flapped from the wireless aerial. I had gone on ahead in the armoured car and now I returned and gave instructions for the convoy to halt. In rather less than half an hour His Highness had shot a fat zebra, a wildebeest, a particularly stupid ostrich which, in fact, buried its head in the sand because it apparently didn't like the sound of the Tchaikovsky violin concerto which was drifting across the plain, and a wart-hog. Whether the music had hypnotized the beasts into an entranced immobility I don't know, but it was only when the reproducer was turned off that they began to show any signs of caring about our presence. But by then we'd got our bait. I spent half an hour arranging the four carcasses in likely positions; then His Highness and I went off on a filming expedition which occupied the rest of the day. Next morning we went out to examine the baits. As we approached, a vast number of carrion feeders—mainly marabout storks and vultures—flapped noisily into the air from the trees. Evidently they were waiting for the king of beasts to finish feeding. We found the wart-hog, the zebra and the wildebeest more or less intact except for the peckings and tearings of vultures;

but the ostrich was at that very moment engaging the attention of two heavily maned lions.

'There you are,' I said; 'the proof of the preference is in the choice.'

The lions backed away a little, their bellies sagging and their faces and manes a mess of blood and filth. There was no doubt at all which kind of flesh they enjoyed. And as His Highness got his ciné camera turning the larger lion decided that he didn't intend any doubt to arise as to present ownership of the bird. He picked the scraggy remains up in his mouth and made off, the great wings and grotesquely thin legs trailing in the dust. Some of our attendant Masai warriors went in pursuit hoping to capture the plumes for the ceremonial headdress, but neither lion would stand for such treatment and they easily outpaced the natives.

The *safari* went on day after day and week after week. We had already covered many hundreds of miles but there seemed no limit to the Maharajah's enthusiasm any more than to his time and money. Ivory, horns, pelts and curiosities of all kinds were sent back by special messengers for treatment by taxidermists in Nairobi. Some specimens were interesting enough for presentation to the museum. And now that His Highness had done most of the shooting he'd looked forward to, he spent more and more time in filming. He had a very artistic eye for the arrangement of a picture and never failed to notice groupings of elephants, buffaloes, or any other creatures which were satisfying in themselves. Time and again he tried to get a picture of lions gathered with perfect symmetry round their prey, and eventually he was successful. The result was truly remarkable: an impala's carcass formed the centre of a rosette of lions' heads and the lions' bodies, all equally spaced, rayed outward in a perfect geometrical pattern, even the tails were lying straight and flat on the ground.

On another occasion he was able to get a good short film of elephants uprooting trees. There had been a heavy shower of rain and the elephants had moved from cover, since they strongly object to water dripping on them; then, when the shower ended, the beasts returned to the grove as if with one mind for revenge and uprooted a dozen trees in as many minutes. Their method is simple and effective: they simply push with their shoulder and forehead at the trunk of the tree, as near the base as possible, and with a few pushes carrying six tons behind them the tree comes crashing down. The elephant then choosily selects the topmost and most tender shoots, tramples the rest of the tree to destruction, and goes on its way rejoicing. This is very well in wild forest land where acacias grow in thousands, but when the destruction is wrought on coconut palms which have taken many years to mature, farmers take a different view.

We now planned the last stage of the grand *safari*. I suggested that it would be a good idea to make our way over the border and back into Kenya and join the main Nairobi–Mombasa road at the famous Sultan Hamud Ranch, where I had once spent that remarkable night when the elephants had destroyed the power-house. From there the whole convoy would move south down the road to Mombasa, where everything would be loaded for the return journey across the Indian Ocean. We would take what adventure came our way on the road but would not deviate far into the land on either side. This seemed to be the sort of triumphal procession the Maharajah might enjoy, and when I outlined the plan to him he was delighted.

We spent a couple of days in the neighbourhood of Moshi, and got some magnificent pictures of Kilimanjaro; then we moved up across the Nyiri Desert to Sultan Hamud.

At the ranch we waited for the convoy to assemble and

were lucky enough to be around when one of the farmers shot a large raiding elephant. The local natives were clamouring for the meat and the farmer decided that the best way to transport the carcass from the close cover where it had been killed to the farm was by tractor. The first thing the tractor driver did was to attach ropes to two of the elephant's rigid legs, then haul away till the great beast was rolled over on to its back and had all its legs and its trunk pointing skyward. Then the ropes were fixed again and the dead elephant was dragged the two miles to the farm in this grotesque manner, with native children running alongside and clambering on to the carcass and holding on to the legs as if they were propelling a gondola. The Maharajah said: 'They're insensitive, these people. To kill the elephant would have been enough. There was no need to drag it through the dust in this undignified manner.' I agreed with him; but I pointed out that the natives' object was the purely practical one of getting the body from one place to another by the easiest means available. Their aesthetic sense didn't run to the consideration of dignity in death.

Radio and telegraphic messages were flying to and from Mombasa. So many arrangements had to be made. It was like transporting an army overseas. And at the same time the Maharajah's subjects at home had to have a daily bulletin of his activities and know all the details of the *safari*. Weeks later I received copies of the relevant newspapers from India and it was all there: quite astonishing to relive those many weeks and find everything so very accurately described.

We had great difficulty in finding enough water to fill our mobile storage tanks for the journey. All around the Sultan Hamud area there had been a prolonged drought and this was now beginning to have its effect. Very few game animals were to be seen, for they had begun to move eastwards towards the Athi in search of water. The evidence was all there. Elephants had found insufficient food for their needs because so much foliage had died off, and one could see where they had attacked the bark of the baobab trees in desperation, ripping the fibrous skin off with their tusks and leaving the trunks naked and white for ten or more feet of their height. And whenever we sent parties of native labourers off to dig in the sandy beds of streams in search of deep-lying water, wild bees clustered round every puddle and gourd. We decided to make do with the absolute minimum and take in further supplies when we came to Tsayo, where the Athi flows towards Lugard's Falls and water would be plentiful.

All the hands from the numerous farms on the ranch had heard of our departure and had decided to make an occasion of it. How this was viewed by authority I don't know; but most employers realize the wisdom of turning a Nelson eye on spontaneous holidays now and again. Anyway they allowed things to take their course and indeed farmers, overseers and administrative people all turned up in force. It was an international occasion, for not only were there natives of a dozen or more different African tribes and races, but representatives of many other nations were there as well: French and Italian mechanics, farmers from New Zealand, Australia and Canada, Indian storekeepers and their staffs, English and German settlers, a missionary or two from Ireland, a Goanese doctor and his Haitian wife, and even a Welsh poet who had settled in Kenya thirty years before but had never forgotten the bardic chair he had won at the Eisteddfod and who sensed an opportunity to voice his pride.

When the convoy was at last ready to move off the Maharajah said he would like to say good-bye to all these good people who had come to see him off. Unbeknown to me he had learnt a little speech in Swahili and this he now broadcast over the electrical reproducer.

The natives, who up to now had been excitedly running up and down the convoy examining every vehicle in detail, were so astonished at the sound of his voice booming out at them from the trumpet affair on the roof of the wireless van that his opening words were lost in cries of wonder and fear. But when I pointed out to them that the disembodied voice really belonged to His Highness, whom they could see through the open door of the caravan, and that he was bidding them farewell, they listened with the most intense attention. The native Masai women giggled and held their babies aloft, and the warriors· got themselves into little groups and shuffled their feet as if with embarrassment. But there was no doubt that they were most impressed and pleased.

His Highness's speech was very brief and Swahili admits of few fine phrases, but his voice was warm with sincerity—a quality which translates into any language. He had arranged for the distribution of gifts—knick-knacks, rolls of coloured cotton cloth, shells, metal mirrors and the like, and when he had finished speaking a great scramble for these took place. The air was loud with laughter and admiration, and startled birds took off in clouds from the loftier trees. Then the Welsh poet stepped forward from somewhere in the crowd and recited *Recessional* in a fine lilting voice which gained no attention from the crowd and I think mildly astonished the Maharajah, but which was well meant. His Highness gracefully acknowledged the address and gave the signal to start. One of the engineers in the wireless van put on a record of Suppé's *Morning, Noon and Night* overture, pariah dogs began to yap and howl, the murmuration of native voices rose to a frenzy—and we were off.

We had some 250 miles to cover, but the road was a good one and we had three days to complete the journey in, so we had no need to speed. In fact, for the first two or three miles while we were getting into our stride the natives ran and scrambled along the road beside us, keeping up an excited chorus of approval and farewell. When I looked back I could see the older and less agile ones thinning out as they gave up the struggle and sitting at the roadside to consider our departure in comfort. But at each village we came to there was always excitement and a gathering.

We camped that night at Mtito Andei, and already the terrain was noticeably greener where tributary streams of the Athi flowed towards us from the Chyulu mountains. Game animals began to appear again, and indeed I had the good fortune to spot a topi antelope with a yellow coat instead of the more usual chestnut colour. It had come down to the stream to drink at dusk and took no more notice of us than it would have of another of its kind. His Highness quickly set up his colour ciné apparatus and photographed it as it drank and galloped off in its ungainly way.

The evening and the night were superb—enchanted with stars and a hunter's moon, cool with the promise of rain. As the sun went down we saw a flight of eagles take off from the tall sycamores that surrounded a nearby pool and head for the distant slopes of Kilimanjaro. A splendid feast of goat's flesh was prepared and we ate in a big marquee pitched beside the road and illuminated by hundreds of coloured bulbs strung on portable lightweight pylons. The low table was laid with gold-crested English china and bowls of fruit. His Highness sat on the carved chair that had been brought from his caravan, wearing a gorgeous silk robe, and with the jewel in his turban flashing like fire.

He did not, of course, drink wine; but he arranged for a wonderful flow of music and conversation to accompany the meal. I can still evoke in my mind the strange feeling of impermanence that attended us while he spoke lightly of the *safari* and of his great triumph in losing a stone in weight, the while Holst's *Planets* worked their cosmic spell in the air. I had a brief feeling that all life on earth was being magically equated with a creation far beyond our comprehension. But there was nothing I can really explain. Let it be.

'Hunter, this has all been very successful, thanks to you. Tell me of your plans.'

'Plans? But I have no plans.'

'To go home?'

I smiled. He had supposed that perhaps I was here in Africa subduing a longing to return to Scotland and that now I had acquired an enormous fee I should have my heart's desire.

I explained how once Hilda and I had gone to Scotland for a visit and I had been chased by a bull and had almost taken a rifle out to shoot it when Hilda had reminded me that we were in a civilized country and that farmers didn't appreciate mad African white hunters shooting their prize beasts.

'It was that "civilized" that did it. And the fact that the country had grown smaller. I seemed to be able to span Scotland with a single glance.'

'But a man's birthplace——'

'Yes,' I said. 'A man's country is his own, and his language, and his native air. But his home is where he makes it, and he's like an ambassador—he carries his own bit of his own country around with him.'

I showed him one of my many snuff boxes, the one I carry with me always. I had a fine watch-glass fitted to it and when you open the lid you can see the dust of moor heather, finer than sand now with so much shifting about as it lies in my pocket, but there for as long as I'm wanting to remember Scotland and Caerlaverock church with the smell of the harvest offerings; a long time.

'Like Chopin and the cup of Polish earth,' he said.

Which I knew nothing of, but I daresay it was an apt remark.

I lay in my sleeping bag that night thinking that this had been a very glamorous *safari* indeed. I could hear the distant cackling of hyenas and some elephants slaking their thirst at the stream. I tried to calculate the miles we had covered, but they were beyond calculation in my sleepy state. I remember falling asleep with a kind of trick film of Kenya flickering in my mind. There was a map, and rhinos and lions kept jumping through it like circus animals through paper hoops. I suppose one of them jumped on me in the end, for I recall no more.

In the morning we were on the move quite early. The lights and tents were all stored again, a loud whine came from the generator van; I had irreverent thoughts about three-ring circuses packing up and moving on, but they were not malicious thoughts—there was no sense in being a Maharajah and not behaving like one.

We had gone only a mile or so when we came on a remarkable scene: a lion pursued by a pack of wild dogs—twenty or more of them yapping and yelping as they tried with wolfish cunning to manœuvre the lion into cover where they could surround him.

Hyenas are cowardly robbers, and vultures scavenge disgustingly, but of all the predatory pests of Africa I think the wild dog is the most despicable and the most merciless. These brindled, mangy beasts with their long fangs and tufted tails hunt in packs or singly, but they never fail to choose a victim they can hound to death while their long 'hoo-hoo-hoo' howl fades over the plain causing consternation most of all among domestic stock and all species of antelope. Lions, cheetahs and leopards always kill their victims before eating them; but wild dogs rip their prey to pieces while still on the run, their fangs tearing off strips of flesh every time they overtake the victim, which loses so much blood and experiences

such agony that escape is impossible. The hounds devour
every scrap of flesh and entrail and then move off in their
relentless way to pick up the trail of the next unfortunate
beast that is to be hounded to death. Single dogs—and
hyenas—will attack domestic stock at night; one of
their favourite tricks being to go for new-born calves and
for the udders of cows, which they rip to pieces with their
teeth and claws, leaving the poor beasts fit for nothing
but a merciful death. As for the antelope world—
especially the lesser kudu, for the flesh of which scavenging dogs have a special passion—these graceful creatures
will seek even human protection in their flight from the
pursuer. I have known an impala to divert its course
and run towards me, its hindquarters ripped away, so
that I could quickly shoot its pursuer; but alas! the
antelope itself also had to be despatched.

The Maharajah had decided to film the pursuit of the
lion if possible to its horrid and inevitable end. 'The
barbarity and wastefulness of nature is something we talk
about glibly but aren't often able to demonstrate. This
looks like the opportunity.'

As it happened, the pursuit was already nearing its
end. We followed the chase for only a few hundred yards
in the armoured car when the lion was brought to bay.
It had probably run for many miles across the veldt and
had now reached the limits of endurance. The dogs, on
the other hand, seemed inexhaustible. And now the
leading half dozen fanned out and sped ahead of the
lion, turning in to face him with their fangs glistening
and their patchy coats bristling. He pulled up and
changed direction; but the pack had closed in at the
sides too. All around him dogs were crouched, slavering.
There was no escape. Magnificent in anger, he roared
once and backed under a thorn tree, snarling and lashing
the ground with his tail.

The dogs closed in slowly. One would make a move

and draw another snarling repulse from the lion which
would halt it and flatten it to the ground with its ears
pressed back as if in cowardly fear. But each dog knew
only too well that the fight was won. And so it proved.
Five of the dogs suddenly made a concerted attack. One
of them was immediately crushed to death by a blow of
the lion's forearm, but the others, snarling, tore and
ripped at his hindquarters and retreated again a little
distance, their fangs slavering with blood and torn flesh,
the smell of which was enough to induce the entire pack
to rush in. They attacked in this manner again and again,
avoiding the blows of the lion's paws with much cunning, until his efforts began to wane. The king of beasts
was being eaten alive, a melancholy and disgusting sight.
Nor was he the only victim: the dog he had slaughtered
was quickly set on and ripped to pieces by its canni-
balistic companions, and there was considerable fighting
among themselves for the tastier bits of offal which were
being ripped from the dying body of the lion. A number
of smaller conflicts between individual dogs were going
on all round, and when eventually the pack made off,
leaving little but the bones and mane of the dead beast,
many of the dogs were themselves limping and bleeding
profusely, and one of them, its belly ripped, collapsed a
little way off but still could not subdue its own lust and
began pulling and snuffling at its own entrails until it
died.

The Maharajah watched and filmed all this with a
stoicism which only just overcame the revulsion he
clearly was experiencing.

'I'm revolted, but not sorry I've had this opportunity,
Hunter.'

I could see that His Highness was thinking that the
splendours and miseries of humanity were equalled by
the contrasting magnificence and cruelty of animal life.
It is often said that the cruelties perpetrated by man are

unequalled in the animal kingdom, and that although animals kill they always do so mercifully. Such thinking is, of course, distorted by sentimentality and has no objective truth. To witness a scene such as I have just described, or to see a hyena attack and eat alive a whelping antelope, is salutary in its horror.

We returned and joined the convoy. Hundreds of Colibus monkeys, terrified of the yelping dogs, had taken to the trees and they now gave us a chattering send-off. These pleasant little creatures were apparently highly delighted by the display of vehicles spread out before them. Their faces as we moved off were like the faces of so many inquisitive old ladies peeping bright-eyed through the foliage and withdrawing in embarrassment when anyone looked up at them. Then as we puffed and snorted on our way they grasped fistfuls of leaves and threw them down like confetti at a wedding.

At Kyulu, where we halted to take in more water from a stream which bubbled delightfully only a few hundred feet from the road, a stock owner came and asked the Maharajah's secretary if I could be spared for a few minutes to come and verify that one of his prize cows had been killed by a marauding lion. The farmer was irately trying to claim damages and tax relief and the inspector wanted an independent opinion as to the cause of the cow's death. His official position demanded that he should be satisfied on that score before the authorities paid out any compensation.

Now a lion is master of the kill, whatever beast it is pursuing as prey. They invariably spring with uncanny accuracy on to the victim's back, turn its head sharply to one side and thus cause it to stumble and break its own neck in falling. Lions inflict this instantaneous death on buffalo, zebra, giraffe, ox or any other mobile prey, and have brought to a fine art the ability to leap clear themselves as their victims' bodies tumble so that they are never crushed by a carcass weighing perhaps a ton or more.

So when the farmer's cow was shown to me and I found myself unable to raise its head from the ground I knew the neck had not been broken.

'Sorry,' I said. 'No lion caused this death.'

For a moment I thought the farmer was going to develop apoplexy; but after a great effort of self-control he calmed down—realizing that anger would get him nowhere.

'Then how——?'

'I don't know yet. Call some of your boys to turn the body over and we may find out.'

He sent for natives and sure enough as soon as the carcass was raised I saw that there was a small bullet hole fizzing away with bubbles of escaping gas.

What had happened, he soon ascertained, was that the watch guard, hearing a night marauder and knowing that a marauding lion was in the vicinity, had shot at something moving near the cow byre and had killed the farmer's best milker in error. Anyway, the farmer was sporting enough to apologize for his bad temper and mistake, offered the inspector and me refreshment and sent us on our way rejoicing.

News of the Maharajah's approach had, of course, gone to Mombasa and it had been decided that he should have a civic reception. All day long messages were passing to and fro on the wireless and His Highness's secretary was continually being consulted about questions of protocol, presentations and the like. The Maharajah smiled a little sadly and said, 'Hunter, this is the last you will see of me.'

I thought for a moment he was about to take off into the air on some secret pocket flying machine, but it turned out that what he meant was that from now on he had to take on the cares of state once more and resume his royal dignity in practice as well as theory. For many weeks he had been comparatively free from the rigid formality of the court, and although his impressive retinue had been in constant attendance, with the unwieldy vehicles of the convoy seeming in many ways ludicrous in big game country, it had been a token of grandeur from which he could easily dissociate himself as a man. Now the grand *safari* was over and he must be a royal ruler once more in every sense of the word.

Civic dignitaries—and the town band—were sent to meet us two miles from the town. The caravan had been turned into a miniature throne room, with the Maharajah sitting impassively in his gorgeous robes, and there Her Majesty's representative was presented. I was not, of course, present at this ceremony and I remember thinking that now the *safari* was really over everything seemed to be slipping away from me. There was a remoteness, an unreality, about all this which was not on my wavelength at all. My task was over and I wished I had not had to come quite this far. I should have bade the Maharajah farewell at Kyulu and gone back to my game ranging; but that, of course, would have been impossibly discourteous. But while the Maharajah was engaged on his ceremonious occasions I drove out to some of the low-lying swampy country round Mombasa and renewed my acquaintance with some of the creatures I dislike most in Africa—mosquitoes, scorpions and lizards of poisonous aspect and malicious intent, hairy tarantulas that come plaguing you in the night, and those urinating pests the bats which haunt the trees in thousands. This land is poor in game and rich in disease-carrying insects, and I've avoided it whenever possible. But it suited my mood like a dying fall of trumpets, and I returned to Mombasa gloomily wondering when I should be able to return to Makindu and get on with some work again.

I was fortunate. The Maharajah had realized that I must now feel rather like a fish out of water and had chartered a plane to fly me back to Nairobi. I scarcely saw him again. The convoy had all been loaded on to the ship and he himself went aboard the day before she sailed and attended to affairs that already were reaching out from India and demanding his attention. He drove to the quay in a magnificent Rolls Royce that had already been furnished with lion skin rugs and upholstery selected from the pelts he had shot himself. I caught a glimpse of him from the road, looking impassively straight ahead as he left Africa behind him. The town band played tinkling teashop tunes and I thought with a smile of how Rachmaninoff in C minor had belted away in opposition to the night noises of the forest and of His Highness complaining that trigger work on his Purdey was bad for passage work on his Scriabin.

Well, a splendid client had come and gone and there was nothing for me to do now but say my farewells to a few people I knew in Mombasa and board my plane. As we took off the vast expanse of the Yatta plateau lay spread out below me. A pair of rare sable antelopes trotted away across the plain and we rose higher and higher until presently there was nothing to be distinguished but a land of solitude. Even the snows of Kilimanjaro were invisible. Wisps of cloud floated by and the din of the engines made me sleepy.

My mood of depression had not really left me. Cut off from the earth like this I felt like a man lost. The solitude of the skies is not for me. It kept occurring to me that everything was over—ridiculously, for in an hour or two I should land again and everything would be the same as it has been for so many years; the threads would be there, waiting to be gathered up. But I was idle there in that comfortable seat; there was no gun to be cleaned, nothing to engage my skill or challenge my senses. If

there had been anybody to be snappy with I'm sure I
should have been very snappy indeed.

Then, just as I was fading off into a disagreeable sort
of doze I suddenly realized exactly what was the matter
with me: I was plainly and simply tired. It had been a
long *safari* and a grand one, but it had taken its toll in a
physical weariness that was just beginning to be notice-
able.

Having found the cause the effect seemed no longer
significant. Of course, everything would be there again—
the heat, the space, the inhospitable bush; the eternal
telegraph messages with their terse appeals to 'kill
dangerous rhino urgent'; the native boys with their wide
grins; and Hilda, waiting. We would drink together as
we always do when I come home and I would sleep for
perhaps twelve hours straight off and then begin all over
again.

So now, for the short duration of this journey, I
wouldn't bother to sleep at all. I would save it all up to
wallow in at home. The sleep of the hunter home from
the hills has always seemed to me a just sleep and as I
thought of its luxury now in my austerely determined
wakefulness I recalled—as I have recalled many times—
the voice of my mother crooning me softly to sleep with
an old Scottish hunting song:

> *O Mother, O Mother,*
> *O make my bed soon,*
> *For I'm weary with huntin'*
> *And fain would lie doun.*

(1)